CULTURE SHOCK!

New Zealand

Peter Oettli

Graphic Arts Center Publishing Company
Portland, Oregon

In the same series

Argentina	*Ecuador*	*Laos*	*South Africa*
Australia	*Egypt*	*Malaysia*	*Spain*
Austria	*Finland*	*Mauritius*	*Sri Lanka*
Belgium	*France*	*Mexico*	*Sweden*
Bolivia	*Germany*	*Morocco*	*Switzerland*
Borneo	*Greece*	*Myanmar*	*Syria*
Brazil	*Hong Kong*	*Nepal*	*Taiwan*
Britain	*Hungary*	*Netherlands*	*Thailand*
California	*India*	*New Zealand*	*Turkey*
Canada	*Indonesia*	*Norway*	*UAE*
Chile	*Iran*	*Pakistan*	*Ukraine*
China	*Ireland*	*Philippines*	*USA*
Costa Rica	*Israel*	*Portugal*	*USA—The South*
Cuba	*Italy*	*Saudi Arabia*	*Venezuela*
Czech Republic	*Japan*	*Scotland*	*Vietnam*
Denmark	*Korea*	*Singapore*	

Barcelona At Your Door	*Paris At Your Door*	*A Student's Guide*
Beijing At Your Door	*Rome At Your Door*	*A Traveller's Medical*
Chicago At Your Door	*San Francisco At*	*Guide*
Havana At Your Door	*Your Door*	*A Wife's Guide*
Jakarta At Your Door	*Shanghai At Your Door*	*Living and Working*
Kuala Lumpur, Malaysia	*Tokyo At Your Door*	*Abroad*
At Your Door	*Vancouver At Your Door*	*Personal Protection At*
London At Your Door		*Home & Abroad*
Moscow At Your Door	*A Globe-Trotter's Guide*	*Working Holidays*
Munich At Your Door	*A Parent's Guide*	*Abroad*
New York At Your Door		

Illustrations by TRIGG

Front cover photograph by New Zealand Tourism Board
Back cover photograph by Lonely Planet Images

Inside photographs by Nick Conway (pages 7, 9, 25, 85, 100, 108, 110, 114, 116, 156, 165, 166, 168, 182, 184), Peter Oettli (pages 26, 39, 44, 51, 55, 66, 68, 72, 74, 82, 105, 112, 133), Sarah Oettli (page 119), Mike Whitaker (page 179), and Benjamin Yap (pages 173, 174).

This book is published by special
arrangement with Marshall Cavendish International (Asia) Pte Ltd
Times Centre, 1 New Industrial Road, Singapore 536196
International Standard Book Number 1-55868-784-X
Library of Congress Catalog Number 2003-103347
Graphic Arts Center Publishing Company
P.O. Box 10306 • Portland, Oregon 97296-0306 • (503) 226-2402

Printed in Singapore

To my wife and family,
who helped and encouraged me along the way.
I am happy and proud to acknowledge them
as my support team.

CONTENTS

Haere Mai 63

Life Down Under 95

ACKNOWLEDGEMENTS

Most books have many authors even though there often is only one name on the title page. This book is no exception. I would like to acknowledge the many friends, acquaintances and work colleagues whom I have pestered for information or questioned about their experiences in coming to live in New Zealand. Their input, so generously given, has been a valuable contribution, and while there are too many of them to mention individually, I would like to express my thanks to them as a group. Individual thanks to Max Oulton for helping with the New Zealand map. Special thanks must go however to my editor, Lynelle Seow, who hounded me mercilessly with questions to ensure that this book is as accurate and up-to-date as it can be. While many of the good points of this book are due to her, any shortcomings are my responsibility.

This book, more than any other book I have written, has also been a family effort. Having grown-up children who now have qualifications in a variety of fields, including business and medicine, has meant that I was able to get first hand information and valuable criticism on various aspects of the text. Special thanks must go to my son-in-law, Nick Conway, for taking the majority of the photographs.

Finally and most importantly, I would like to thank my wife not just for her support and encouragement, but also for her helpful criticism and suggestions. She generously devoted a substantial amount of time to reading the manuscript and her numerous comments, always very tactfully delivered, were most valuable.

So thank you team! For your comments, for your input, for your help and encouragement and just for being there.

INTRODUCTION

Many hundreds of years ago, so the Maori, the original Polynesian inhabitants of New Zealand, tell it, a young man called Maui went fishing with his four older brothers. Somehow he managed to persuade them to go much further south than usual and finally chose a spot where they would lower their hooks. He had a fishing line, but neither hook nor bait, and his brothers refused to let him have any, so he used the jawbone of his grandmother, Murirangawhenua, as a hook and baited it with blood obtained by punching his own nose. The magic hook and the irresistible bait worked wonders. Maui landed an enormous fish – the North Island of New Zealand! This is why one of the ancient names for New Zealand in the Maori language is *Te Ika a Maui* – the fish of Maui. It is one of many names for the beautiful islands in the south of the South Pacific, and all of them reflect an aspect of the country's history. The myth tells us that Maui returned to his homeland, the mythical Hawaiki, and gave his people directions to find what he called *Tiritiri o te Moana*—the Gift of the Sea. The first navigator to come to New Zealand named in Maori tradition is Kupe. He explored the coast of the North Island and was the first to sail through the strait that divides the two main islands. According to some traditions, Kupe also went to the South Island. He left New Zealand from a harbour on the west coast in the north of the North Islands which was named *Hokianga nui a Kupe*—the Great Returning Place of Kupe—a name that has remained on our maps in the abbreviated form of Hokianga. Another poetic name which goes back to the early Polynesian navigators and which is often used as an alternative name for New Zealand is *Aotearoa*—the Land of the Long White Cloud.

The first European navigator to reach and name New Zealand was Abel Tasman. He had been sent by the Dutch East India Company in 1642 to find the hypothetical southern continent full of fabled riches. He set out from Batavia, today's Jakarta, and found New Zealand instead, naming the country after the Dutch province of Zeeland in the Netherlands.

Seeing that Tasman had not found any gold, interest in New Zealand was not strong, and it was over a hundred years later, in 1769, that Captain James Cook came from England on his ship, the *Endeavour*. He visited the islands and proved once and for all that they were just large islands and not the great southern continent whose existence had been assumed by the scholars of his day. Cook charted the islands, both on this voyage and on two other return voyage several years later. During his visits he added many names to the map of New Zealand. The name of the country however, remained New Zealand, and today it is often referred to as Aotearoa/New Zealand. In 1779, Cook, the brilliant navigator and one of New Zealand's heroes met an untimely death. He was killed in an altercation with the local people on the island of Hawaii.

The encounter between the early explorers and the original inhabitants were not always peaceful. Part of the reason was that they did not know each other's language and culture. A number of unfortunate incidents, some of them resulting in the deaths of some of the participants, can be attributed to misunderstandings arising from this ignorance.

Many millions of people have followed in the wake of the first navigators and settlers. Some of them have stayed, some have returned after a visit of some weeks, months or years. Most of them don't travel by boat any more; they arrive by modern aircraft. And most of them are not totally in the dark about what they are going to find once they arrive here. New Zealand has been well and truly charted, and all you need to do is to study the chart or guide before setting out. There are plenty of books about New Zealand, beginning with the record of the early Polynesian migrations and the journals of Captain Cook and the early explorers. Some of them are listed at the end of this book.

This book is designed to help the modern day navigators, explorers and settlers to find their way in modern-day New Zealand. It will give you the information that the early travellers and many of those that followed them did not have and had to find out the hard way. Travel is always an adventure, and travel to an unknown destination is an even greater adventure. This book is designed to help you obtain as much pleasure and profit as possible from the adventure of visiting Aotearoa/New Zealand. Welcome and *kia ora tatou*.

HOW TO GET CULTURE SHOCK IN ONE EASY LESSON . . .

Culture shock, and its associated condition, homesickness, are two related problems that most travellers have suffered to a greater or lesser degree ever since there have been travellers. So you have decided, or your boss or partner has decided, to travel to New Zealand. You may not even know exactly where it is, what kind of people live there, what language they speak, what food they eat? Here is what you can do to maximise your chances of getting culture shock.

Firstly, assume that everything in New Zealand will be like it is where you are now. If you have servants in your household, gardeners, drivers, assume that you will have them in New Zealand. Assume that the food will be exactly like it is where you are now. It will have the same ingredients, it will have the same taste, and you won't even know you are in a different culture. Also assume that the people will be the same. They will know how to behave towards you because you will treat them just as you treat the people around you in your home culture.

Secondly, assume that everything will be exactly how the tourist brochures have described it. Assume that the skies will always be a deep azure blue, that clearly there never is any bad weather, that there will be lots and lots of eager people waiting to cater to your every whim (for a very reasonable price!), and that there are flocks of clean and sanitised sheep grazing on Auckland airport in between takeoffs and landings. Also assume that friendly Maori in grass skirts will conduct you around boiling mudpools anywhere in New Zealand, unless there are snowcapped mountains and volcanoes where you will go skiing and mountaineering. Assume that there will be an endless round of extreme sports, that New Zealanders spend most of their time roaring up and down rivers in jet boats, hurling themselves out of aeroplanes or diving head first from a bungee jumping platform from a great height, or doing daredevil stunts on surfboards on the breaking faces of gigantic waves.

Finally, assume that while everybody else you know has suffered from culture shock and the associated homesickness, you are totally immune to both. You are going to be totally unaffected because you are not expecting any major differences between the culture you are in now and New Zealand culture, and anyway, the tourist brochures have told you that the sun always shines in New Zealand, that life here is one big round of excitement, fun and entertainment, so how on earth would you encounter culture shock. You are the invincible traveller!

... AND HOW TO DEAL WITH IT WHEN IT STRIKES

You will have noticed that I did not say 'if' it strikes, but 'when' it strikes. There are degrees of culture shock, and not everybody is affected to the same degree. But it will strike, and the more immune you may think you are to culture shock, the harder it will strike because in addition to culture shock and homesickness, you will also be shocked by the realisation that you were not the invincible traveller after all. But fortunately there are ways to cope with the shock, and here are a few strategies to help you to do so.

It is important that you recognise culture shock when it strikes. I did not recognise it when I first arrived in New Zealand, and yet it struck on the second day. In my home country, Switzerland, I had been used to a modern, clean, very efficient and comfortable rail system. After a sleepless night in an ancient carriage on the express train from Wellington, we were met at Frankton Station by an old farm truck that was to take us to the farm that my parents had bought. I still vividly remember standing on the station platform waiting for the truck, watching primitive double-decker sheep wagons full of smelly sheep being shunted around, getting wet in the frequent showers that lashed the station on that November morning and staring gloomily into a bleak cityscape that seemed to consist only of factories and sooty workshops.

I now realise that I was quite depressed at the time and I now also realise that depression is one of the signs of culture shock. It can strike at any time. It can strike in the first day or two, as it did with me. You arrive, and find that the surroundings are totally different from what you expected, or that the arrangements have somehow unravelled and you hastily have to find alternatives. Or else, the arrangements work fine but are not satisfactory. Many years later, I remember moving to a different country with my family for the purpose of a short sabbatical and renting an apartment before leaving New Zealand. When we arrived, it turned out that the apartment was miles out of town and the nearest shop was a 45-minute walk away. In addition, it was winter, with daylight only between 9:00 a.m. and 3:30 p.m. and bitter cold. Enough to make you depressed even if you lived there!

Sometimes, culture shock strikes later, when all the excitement of arrival and settling in has subsided and the routine of everyday life shows up flaws in what you had at first thought was a brilliant country. You begin to see and be irked by the less desirable aspects of the new culture. Some people become almost obsessed with them and in their minds they become exaggerated, just as the good points of the country they left become also magnified.

If you are depressed and find yourself thinking all the time of how much better everything was at home, you are suffering from culture shock. Also, if you continually brood on the question whether it was really a good idea to come to the new country, you may be suffering from culture shock. Fortunately there are things you can do initially to minimise it and then to cope with it.

Firstly, before you set out on your travels, get as much reliable information about the country that you are going to visit. Don't be taken in by tourist brochures. They have one purpose only: to sell the country and to entice as many people as possible to come and visit. So they will paint a rosy picture that may have some connection with the reality that you will encounter, but it is important that you get balanced information that goes beyond the glossy booklets. This book will give you practical and balanced information as well as pointers to where you can get more. These days, the Internet will often have up-to-the-minute figures. This is the reason why I normally do not give prices. You will be able to get the most recent ones from the websites listed in the *Resource Guide* at the end. But make sure that you get as much information as you can, check it against other sources, and be aware that different publications have different aims. If you know people who have been to New Zealand, go and talk to them. But beware! Some of them may have been in the country as tourists and may not have lived in it for any length of time. So again, you may be able to get valuable and helpful information from friends and acquaintances, but cross-check your information.

Here is a small example of how easy it is to get wrong information. When we were thinking about immigrating to New Zealand, a Swiss who had done so and was back in Switzerland came to visit us one evening to talk about his new adopted country. He insisted that there were absolutely no flies in New Zealand! We believed him, of course; after all he had lived there and was the expert. He could not have been more wrong, especially in a milking shed on a hot summer's evening! In the event, it did not matter that we had been misled, but it pays to verify any information if you can.

Secondly, don't come to New Zealand with unrealistic expectations. While many things will be very similar to the way they were in your home country, there will be many differences. If you have unrealistic expectations, you are bound to be disappointed and as we have seen, this can subtly poison your whole experience. Again, this book is intended to help you get a realistic picture of New Zealand and its people. These expectations may relate to the weather—there are wet, cold, miserable days in New Zealand; or to the social structure—you will not be able to have servants in New Zealand; or to the transport system—public transport is not frequent in New Zealand. Again, this book will give you the information you need to avoid having unrealistic expectations.

Thirdly, be prepared to be flexible and adaptable. There will be many instances where you would like things to be different, but they are not. New Zealanders are easy-going people; in fact, their casual approach to things can be quite a shock to those people who come from a more formal society. But it does mean that most of them are reasonable if they see you being reasonable. Be prepared to give and take, learn to laugh at your occasional mistakes, and you will lessen the culture shock considerably.

Fourthly, maintain contacts with your family in your home country and establish contacts with your cultural community here in New Zealand. If you don't have any contacts with people from your home country here in New Zealand, this book will show you how to go about establishing some. People from your home country who have lived in New Zealand for some time can often be a great help. They have experienced culture shock and have developed ways of coping with it that will be appropriate to your culture.

So be prepared to encounter culture shock and be prepared to deal with it when it occurs. Hopefully this book will help you. It is designed as a culture shock absorber.

Chapter One

OVERVIEW

FROM NORTH CAPE TO THE BLUFF

Although it is now a long time ago, I still remember looking for New Zealand in my parents' atlas when they told us children that they were thinking of emigrating from Switzerland to New Zealand. It was Knaur's Atlas, a German edition that had been published before the end of the Second World War, and Hitler's and Mussolini's conquests were incorporated in the redrawn maps of Europe and Africa. New Zealand was not easy to find. It was on one of the last pages of the atlas, and on the same page with Australia. It looked tiny!

Measured against the vastness of the Pacific, and against its neighbour Australia (which is about 29 times the size of New Zealand), the country does indeed look small. But it is all a matter of perspective. With its land area of more than 268,000 square kilometres (103,500 square miles), New Zealand is a bit larger than the United Kingdom, a bit more than two thirds the size of Japan and almost three times the size of South Korea.

It is a long country. The two main islands and Stewart Island to the south extend over 1600 km (994 miles). This roughly corresponds to the distance from Berlin to Moscow or from Hong Kong to Calcutta. It is also a country of mountains and rolling hills. The Southern Alps (named after the European Alps by their Austrian explorer) form the backbone of the South Island with Mount Cook, the highest mountain in New Zealand—at 3764 m (12,400 feet)—at its peak. The centre of the North Island is dominated by three volcanoes: Ruapehu, Tongariro and Ngauruhoe. A fourth volcano, Mt. Taranaki, sits in solitary splendour in the Taranaki province, on the west coast of the North Island. The Maori tell the story of all four volcanoes living together in the centre of the North Island. Tongariro married a lovely little mountain called Pihanga. The problem was that Taranaki also loved Pihanga. When Tongariro discovered this, he became angry and drove Taranaki westwards with great fire. The fleeing Taranaki carved the Wanganui River valley before he came to rest on the coast. When you fly between Auckland or Hamilton and Wellington, you can see for yourself on a clear day how lonely and forlorn poor Taranaki looks.

Volcanoes

Apart from four large volcanoes, there are dozens of smaller ones. White Island, off the eastern coast of the North Island, still smokes on the horizon when you look out to sea from Whakatane. New Zealand's largest city, Auckland, has about 50 (hopefully extinct) volcanoes dotted throughout the city. The youngest volcano, Rangitoto, erupted

a mere 600 years ago and is now an island in Auckland harbour. I have walked on it and found that, while it is covered in vegetation, it still has a very thin layer of topsoil. Much of the island is covered in black basalt rocks.

Lakes

Beautiful lakes are also a feature of both the South Island and the centre of the North Island, where you find the largest of the New Zealand lakes, Lake Taupo, occupying 606 square kilometres (234 square miles) of a volcanic crater. The eruption that formed the crater is probably the world's largest volcanic eruption in the last 7000 years and occurred about 1800 years ago. Historians in China and Rome recorded details of deep red sunsets and darkened daily skies from the ash that was hurled 50 km (31 miles) up into the atmosphere. The resulting lake is about the same size as Singapore.

Earthquakes

While we are talking about eruptions, New Zealand is infamous. The New Zealand Institute of Geological and Nuclear Sciences records about 14,000 earthquakes every year in and around New Zealand. Most of them are too small to be noticed, but between 100 and 150 can be felt a year. The reason for all this shaking is due to the movements of the Pacific and the Australian plates grinding against each other. The first earthquake that I experienced is memorable because I almost missed it. I was outside our farmhouse when suddenly my mother and sister came running out, claiming they had felt the house shake. I had felt nothing because I was outside, but when we went back in, we found some crockery that had fallen out of the rack and crashed to the floor. In case you need advice about how to act in earthquakes and volcanic eruptions, the Ministry of Civil Defence instructions are printed inside the cover of the New Zealand Telephone Directory. In the event that you don't have a telephone directory handy when a quake strikes, the basic rule is to stay indoors and take cover under a sturdy table.

Winds

Wherever you are in New Zealand, you are never far from the sea. I live in the inland city of Hamilton in the North Island. From here, it takes 45 minutes to drive to the west coast, and a bit over an hour to enjoy the beaches of the east coast. Young people in Hamilton who are interested in surfing don't have to wait for a suitable wind. When it blows from the west, they drive to Manu Bay in Raglan, some 48 km (30 miles) west of Hamilton, to experience the world's longest and most consistent left-hand break. This break, which was featured in the 1966 cult classic film *Endless Summer*, attracts surfers from all over the world. When the Raglan waters are smooth because there is an easterly wind, they simply drive over to Mount Maunganui on the east coast where there is bound to be a good surf running as long as there is wind to make the waves, of course.

The south of the North Island and the whole South Island are situated in an area that is known as the Roaring Forties. This area is characterized by strong westerly winds, which old sailors took advantage of to drive their ships from New Zealand towards Cape Horn on their journey back to Europe. Wind conditions however are usually moderate, although they may change more frequently than in many other regions in the world. Some parts of the country experience more breezy conditions than others, such as windy Wellington.

I fly to the capital fairly frequently and, as far as I am concerned, Wellington has one of the most exciting airports in the world. There, landing sideways seems to be a speciality of the Air New Zealand pilots. It is the only airport where, sitting in the rear of the aircraft, I have actually watched the cabin flex sideways after takeoff because we were buffeted by violent wind gusts. It has not deterred me from visiting Wellington frequently. New Zealand pilots are superb, and I have absolute confidence in them. (Just in case you think that this confidence is misplaced, by the time you read this, I am sure I will have flown into and out of Wellington several dozen times with lots of exciting bumps but no mishaps!)

Climate

While there clearly are variations in climatic conditions between the north of the North Island and the southern extremity of the South Island, the climate is generally described as temperate. There are parts of Northland that never experience frosts, even at night in winter. The Alpine regions of the South Island, on the other hand, can get as cold as −12°C (10°F) in winter. The average temperature in the northern part of New Zealand is 15°C (59°F), while in the south, it is cooler at 9°C (48°F).

Of course, one of the climatic features of New Zealand is that, because it is in the Southern Hemisphere, the seasons are reversed. That means that when it is coldest here in July, North America, Europe or North Asia can be sweltering in heatwaves. This also means that shop windows adorned with Christmas decorations and artificial snow will fail to convince the avid European traditionalist that it feels like Christmas when outdoor temperatures are often in the high twenties (low eighties) in December. The hottest months in New Zealand are January and February.

New arrivals in New Zealand have described its weather as unpredictable. In many climates, you can expect the weather to conform to certain patterns. The monsoon rains will come in their appointed season (more or less!), or during the dry season, you know that it will not rain for quite some time; but not so in New Zealand. The weather will change, sometimes several times a day. While there are days and weeks when it is fine, particularly in late summer, days and weeks of just rain or cloud are comparatively rare.

Environment

One of the major attractions of New Zealand is that it is a very beautiful country. It is clean, green and has ever-changing scenery, ranging from coastal panoramas to rolling hills, volcanoes, thermal areas, bush (native forests), pastoral landscapes, glaciers, mountains, lakes and rivers. Every visitor I have talked to has commented on this.

A waterfall in the New Zealand bush.

Because all this wealth of scenic beauty is in a comparatively small country, travel is never boring; the landscape (just like the weather sometimes!) changes every hour or two. The landscape is overwhelmingly rural. Flying over it, you will find that human beings have not yet had the impact on it that they have had in other parts of the world. There are still areas of rugged bush and untouched valleys and ravines. This is a marked contrast to flying over, say Europe, where forests and fields have straight edges. Another contrast is, of course, that in Europe and many parts of Asia, you can find a town or village every few kilometres; in New Zealand towns are far apart. I have often marvelled at the work the early European pioneers did to build the network of roads that serves these scattered, small communities.

Five cities in New Zealand are considered 'major', and even these are small by world standards. Only one, Auckland, home to a third of New Zealand's population, has more than a million inhabitants. You will find that the New Zealand media often talk about the 'four main centres' by which they mean Auckland, Wellington, Christchurch and Dunedin. Hamilton has recently surpassed the population of Dunedin, but old habits die hard and Dunedin continues to be referred to as one of the four main centres. Wellington is the capital of New Zealand and therefore contains the head offices of most ministries as well as foreign embassies.

TANGATA WHENUA AND COLONIST

The Maori people describe themselves as the *tangata whenua*, the people of the land, and they are the original settlers in New Zealand. The first non-Polynesian settlers along the shores of New Zealand were sealers and whalers. Many of these seafarers took Maori 'wives' and their offspring would be the earliest New Zealanders of mixed lineage. With the arrival of increasing numbers of traders and permanent settlers, intermarriage between Maori and *Pakeha* (Europeans) became more common. Most Maori today will tell you of a European forebear

A crowded Auckland street. Auckland is New Zealand's largest city.

in their *whakapapa* (geneology), and many of them are proud of their European *tupuna* (ancestors).

The sealers and whalers were later followed by missionaries, agriculturalists, explorers, merchants and adventurers. In 1837, the New Zealand Association was formed in England, becoming the New Zealand Company in 1839. The organization aimed to colonize New Zealand in accordance with the principles of Edward Gibbon Wakefield, an English theorist. Wakefield sought to establish a British colony in New Zealand based on the English social system. Canterbury is considered the most successful of such settlements.

The British government took a growing interest in New Zealand, and more Europeans settled in the country. By 1839, there were about

2000 *Pakeha* in New Zealand. The rapid growth in the *Pakeha* population alarmed Maori chiefs and tensions escalated. The compromise between the British government and the Maori chiefs culminated in the Treaty of Waitangi, signed on 6 February 1840, at Waitangi in the Bay of Islands. Those Maori chiefs who signed on behalf of their tribes (not all of them did!), ceded sovereignty to the British Queen, who in turn granted them the status of British subjects with all the rights and privileges that came with it. The Queen guaranteed the Maori possession of their lands, fisheries and other possessions. To prevent unscrupulous purchasers from exploiting the Maori, land was to be sold directly to the Crown.

In the same year, the first New Zealand Company settlers arrived in Port Nicholson (today's Wellington) and founded the first settlement. More settlers followed in the next few years, especially between 1840 and 1860. The influx of European settlers pressured the colonial administrators of New Zealand to make more land available. The Maori population, feeling threatened by the ever increasing number of *Pakeha* agitating for more and more land, began to refuse to sell more land. Tensions mounted and erupted in wars throughout the country in the 1860s.

The Maori had reason to feel threatened. The Europeans had brought with them not just ' civilisation', but also firearms, alcohol and diseases against which the Maori population had little or no immunity. With Maori arming themselves with firearms instead of traditional weapons, intertribal raids resulted in more deaths and casualties. The Maori population plummeted as a result of these wars and, above all, disease. Many settlers assumed that the Maori race was dying out. They were wrong. Although it took years for the Maori to regain their numbers and morale, today, about one in seven people in New Zealand are of Maori ethnicity.

Attempts have been made to address the injustices perpetrated in the 1860 wars and their aftermath, particularly with regard to land, as we shall see in the next chapter.

THE NUMBER-8-WIRE MENTALITY

Nine hundred years ago, both the Maori and *Pakeha* settlers had one thing in common; they were pioneers in a land rich in promise. The Maori and *Pakeha* settlers that followed the whalers and sealers were agriculturalists and for both of them, the land offered food in abundance in addition to what they planted and harvested. The sea teemed with fish, and the bird population, which had fed the Maori hunters, had been augmented with the introduction of mammals, some of which roamed the bush and could be hunted for meat. Captain Cook had left some pigs in New Zealand. Some escaped into the wild and multiplied. Therefore even today, Maori and *Pakeha* hunters can bring home Captain Cook's wild pigs for dinner.

The Pioneering Spirit

The pioneering spirit of New Zealanders is still alive and well and expresses itself in many ways. Hunting and fishing in many societies are the preserve of the rich, but in New Zealand, they are considered the right of the ordinary bloke. A *bloke* is the term Kiwis use for the common man.

The ordinary bloke is an uncomplicated fellow normally dressed in shorts and a black singlet (the sleeveless vest worn by many farmers in summer). When he is not out with his mates fishing, hunting, or drinking at the pub, he lurks in his shed at the bottom of the garden, tinkering with his car, sorting out his fishing gear or simply dreaming of the next trip into the bush. He is the sort of fellow who comes home late from the pub, where he has been drinking with his mates, a bit the worse for wear. If he finds that his wife has locked him out, the stereotype dictates that he will go to the shed, get out his chain saw and cut down the front door to get in.

The emphasis on the values and qualities of a pioneering society is beginning to fade, but visitors to the country should be aware that it is still strong. It manifests itself in two ways: firstly, in the country's

11

obsession with sport, particularly rugby, and secondly, in a certain anti-intellectualism. For example, in a typical New Zealand high school, the captain of the most senior rugby team, the 'First Fifteen', far outranks the 'Dux', the top academic student, in terms of social status amongst their peers. It has also been said that the prime minister of New Zealand occupies the third most important position in the country, after the captain and the coach of the national rugby team. Physical prowess, the attribute required to subdue the land and provide food and shelter, is still highly valued.

Egalitarianism

Another value that New Zealanders have inherited from their colonial past is a very strong egalitarianism. Most of the immigrants from Britain and Europe emigrated to better themselves, that is, they wanted to escape from the confines of class and poverty to become the equal of their masters. One of the early visitors to the colony reported her shock at finding that while servants addressed each other by titles, such as Mr and Mrs, they referred to their employers and 'betters' simply by their surnames without the courtesy of a title.

While this shocking state of affairs has not continued into the 21st century (titles are used very rarely, and only on formal occasions), it is important for visitors to New Zealand to be aware of this egalitarianism. It was certainly behind the recent decision of the New Zealand government to depart from the British system of honours accorded to knights, which would entitle the honoured person to preface their name with 'Sir' or 'Dame'. We still have the honours, but the title has been abolished.

Many years ago when I was a junior member of my university, I had occasion to host a senior academic from a European country. I had arranged for a function on one of the evenings that he was at my university, and had invited a cross-section of the institution to the party. After less than an hour, my guest approached me and demanded angrily to be taken to his hotel. The reason for his abrupt wish to depart? All the people who had approached him to talk had been below the rank of a professor! I managed to placate him but it drove home the lesson that New Zealand attitudes to social position, rank and prestige are different from those of many other countries. The important thing to keep in mind is that in New Zealand (and I would like to think everywhere else), you treat every person you deal with, whether he carries your suitcases up to your room or whether she deals with you as a government official or whether they are Cabinet ministers or captains of industry, as a worthwhile individual. They deserve the courtesy and dignity that you expect for yourself. You can't go wrong with that—in any country. It may even help you avoid embarrassment. The first head of the university in which I work was a prominent professor of chemistry before he was appointed as a vice-chancellor of the university. One weekend, he came to the university to pick up some documents from his office dressed in his very informal weekend clothes. A visitor to the university asked him for directions and then for help in carrying some boxes into one of the buildings. The Vice-Chancellor was very happy to help, only he was not, as the visitor thought, one of the caretakers.

Another aspect of the New Zealand egalitarianism is that New Zealanders do not have servants, at least not in the sense of permanent household staff. When my wife and I both worked full-time, we employed cleaning ladies to come and clean the house once a week. We still employ a contractor to mow our lawns regularly. But generally, live-in servants are not part of the New Zealand household. If you are invited to share a meal in a New Zealand home, it would most likely have been cooked by the hostess herself and not by a live-in cook.

As always, there is, of course, the other side of the coin. While the New Zealand egalitarian attitude has many good aspects (it largely removes complicated social rituals that have to do with recognising caste or class distinctions), it has also produced what in New Zealand is called the Tall Poppy syndrome. The term refers to the fact that

Kiwis who stand out are often cut down by the mediocre. This means that those who are more intelligent, performing better than average, making more money, or who are more successful than the rest, are not looked up to as role models. This is discouraging to high performers. It is also partly responsible for the New Zealander's avoidance of ostentation. If you are the kind of person who flamboyantly displays wealth or success, you might get away with it if you are a foreigner on a brief visit. You will then be seen as a rather colourful and eccentric foreign visitor. If you are planning on staying for some time however and becoming part of New Zealand society, try and blend into it. You may still be very successful, but successful Kiwis tend to hide, rather than flaunt, their success. The one exception to this rule is sport. Successful sportspeople in New Zealand very quickly become 'celebrities' and they are allowed to display the symbols of their success with impunity.

Do-It-Yourself

"Girls can do anything!" is one of the watchwords of the feminist movement (and it is with pride that we remind everyone that New Zealand was the first country in the world to give women the right to vote!) It could be applied to all New Zealanders of both genders. Another aspect of the egalitarianism that I have just talked about is that they attempt to do anything—skilled tradespeople are not really needed, as long as you have a few spanners, woodworking tools and a stick of dynamite or two. This attitude, which is the basic attitude of any do-it-yourself (D.I.Y.) enthusiast is very widespread in New Zealand. I read a story in our local paper about a surgeon who rebuilt the inside of his 19th century house. Some years ago, I met a district court judge in his home and at first mistook him for a builder. I had not known he was a judge. When I entered the living room of his home where major alterations were going on, he stepped down from a ladder, dressed in shorts with his hair garlanded with sawdust and wood shavings.

There are countless stores that cater to the D.I.Y. brigade. They don't only sell the materials needed for a D.I.Y. project, but also provide helpful pamphlets on how to do almost anything. So if you want to add a whole new floor to your house, you will be able to find both advice and materials to do it.

I would, however, not advise you to embark on an ambitious project, unless you have had some experience at working with your hands. You will also need to be careful that you find out all about building codes and regulations. Just because you "do it yourself" does not mean that you are exempt from getting the right permits to make alterations to your house. Some Kiwis have made the most dreadful blunders. There is a popular TV programme in New Zealand called *Do-it-Yourself Rescue* in which tradespeople go and remedy some of the botched do-it-yourself projects, and believe me, most of the projects tackled by the rescue team are not a pretty sight!

Again, this do-it-yourself attitude goes back to that pioneering spirit I talked about earlier. A pioneer has no time and cannot afford to wait for the expert, and often there were no experts available anyway. So he or she had to do everything that was necessary to ensure survival. I certainly got hooked into this attitude quite early. While studying at the university and getting my degrees in history and literature, I totally dismantled a motorcycle engine and rebuilt it again (yes, it went fine), crafted some (admittedly, quite crude) furniture for my room and set up an aerial system that gave me excellent reception of all the New Zealand broadcasting stations. Later in life, while I was raising a family and teaching at the university, I built two wooden sailboats; a small one and a larger sailboat, some 6.7 m (22 feet) in length, both of which proved very seaworthy. And I forgot about the concrete paths I poured around our new house and the standard lamp and coffee table I made for our house that are still in use today!

While I am not a native Kiwi, the achievements I have just boasted about would be taken for granted by most New Zealanders. This attitude has been described as the Number-8-wire mentality. It refers to the fact that the most commonly used wire for fences to keep cows and sheep in their paddocks is called Number-8-wire. It is quite thick, and thousands and thousands of kilometres of fence have been built with it. But it can be used for much more than building fences. You can make a coat hanger from it. It can serve as a dipstick to see how much diesel is left in your tractor. My farmer father even made clips from it to keep his old, tatty oilskin raincoat buttoned after the buttons had fallen off. But it does not have to be Number-8-wire. The expression refers to the fact that many New Zealanders have the ability to fix anything with whatever is available.

Perhaps, it even refers to my experience when I was a very young and very new Kiwi driving a truck loaded with bales of hay from my father's farm to my uncle's property. It was a lovely, warm summer evening and I was just getting to the top of a hill when suddenly smoke started to pour from the bonnet of the old truck. I stopped and managed to put out the fire. When I inspected the motor, I discovered that an oil hose had come unstuck and was spraying oil onto the hot manifold, thereby causing the fire. I was no mechanic and had no tools or spare parts. But there were many bales of hay on my truck, and the bales were tied with green twine. I cut off some twine, reattached the hose and tied it up with the green string. The temporary repair got me and my vehicle safely to my destination. Admittedly, truck and car engines were simpler back then. I doubt that a piece of bailing twine could be used to fix one of these modern engines full of computer and electronic gadget wizardry.

Give It a Go!

Another New Zealand value is embodied in the words 'give it a go'. You may not be an expert, but you will be admired for trying, no matter what. I worked in a large paper factory during one of my summer vacations in my student days. One afternoon, I had to run an errand to the part of the factory where the trees were sorted. Huge logs came in on a conveyor and a man sitting in front of a desk with several rows of buttons manipulated them at great speed. With a press of a button, he could 'kick' the logs into various destinations using huge pneumatic rams. I stood behind him admiring the skill with which he handled the process. Suddenly, he got up and motioned me to sit in his place. "Give it a go," he said with a grin. In ten minutes, I had created such a log jam that they had to get a crane from outside to untangle the mess. The workers thought it was a huge joke, but I had, at least, 'given it a go'.

New Zealand vs Australia

New Zealanders are very proud of their country. Don't be surprised if a Kiwi asks you what you think of the country after you have only just arrived. Like the inhabitants of so many smaller countries that are next door to much larger and wealthier nations, New Zealanders get quite offended if foreigners, often out of pure ignorance, imply in any way that New Zealand is part of Australia. While relations between Australia and New Zealand are really very good, there is a love-hate relationship between the two neighbours. Kiwis see Aussies as brash and uncultured, while Australians describe New Zealanders as backward, inbred and naive country peasants. Both make the other the butt of jokes:

> Australian question: Why are so few crimes solved in
> New Zealand?
> Answer: Because all Kiwis have the same DNA.
> Kiwi question: What is the difference between Australia
> and yoghurt?
> Answer: One has a living culture.

Seeing that this is a book about New Zealand, I may be permitted one more story. A Malaysian, an Australian and a Kiwi are caught in an Arab state smuggling rum. They are sentenced to death, but that sentence is later commuted to life imprisonment. On his birthday, the sheik announces an amnesty. The trio will be released after receiving 20 lashes each. But since it is his birthday, the sheik allows each prisoner one wish before the corporal punishment is carried out. The Malaysian goes first, and after some thought, asks for a pillow to be tied to his back. This is done, but the pillow only lasts for five lashes before the whip cuts through. The Aussie comes next and he asks for two pillows to be tied to his back. His two pillows survive for 10 lashes and then again the whip cuts through. Finally, the Kiwi gets his turn. Before he has time to state his wish, the sheik says: "Because you come from such a beautiful country and you have such a good rugby team, I will grant you two wishes."

"Thank you, your most gracious and merciful Highness," replies the Kiwi. "My first wish is to receive not 20, but 40 lashes." The sheik nods his assent, a bit puzzled.

"What is your second wish?"

"My second wish is to tie the Aussie to my back!" replies the Kiwi.

LIVING UPSIDE DOWN

One thing that New Zealanders and Australians share is that they live 'upside down', that is they live in the Southern Hemisphere of the globe, in geographic and, sometimes, geopolitical isolation. I leave someone else to gauge what effect that has had on the Australians— it has certainly affected New Zealanders and the way they live and think.

One of the effects of our isolation is that New Zealanders must be amongst the most frequent international travellers in the world. It starts with the 'OE' (overseas experience) of many young people. After they have finished their education, they work for a while to get together some money, and then they take off, almost always into the Northern Hemisphere, particularly Britain, where they understand the language and can find some temporary work. Some go for just a few months, but many stay a year or two before returning to their home country, richer in experience, and sometimes with a partner.

(They are, after all, in that age bracket where one looks for a partner). But it does not stop there. New Zealanders are inveterate travellers, both for business and for pleasure, and I come across them in all sorts of strange places, doing all sorts of strange things. I remember once sitting in the Air New Zealand lounge in Seoul, talking to a businessman who had just managed to sell several tons of ice cream to Siberia (of all places!) The problem was that Siberia did not have enough refrigerators to store the ice cream, so he was flying home to New Zealand to organize the refrigerators to be shipped to Siberia before the avalanche of ice cream arrived. You will find Kiwis tramping (hiking) in Nepal, driving canal boats in France, herding reindeer in Lapland or collecting orchids in Papua New Guinea. They live in the most beautiful country in the world, but their thirst for adventure will drive them to travel to ever new destinations.

This means that Kiwis are good at geography. If you tell them where you are from, they are very likely to know where your country is and, possibly, have even been there. This is in contrast to the inhabitants of much larger and much more powerful countries in the Northern Hemisphere. I have lost count of the number of people to whom I have had to patiently explain where New Zealand actually is. A typical experience is the one I had recently with a service station attendant in rural Pennsylvania. "Where are you guys from?" she wanted to know when I went to pay for the gasoline.

"New Zealand."

"Oh! Cool," she replied, "my boyfriend bought me a koala from there!"

I am too much of an acclimatised New Zealander not to take offence at the implication that koalas, one of the icons of Australia, come from New Zealand.

Another effect of living at the southern edge of the world in a small country is that New Zealanders are surprisingly well informed about world affairs. I have read newspapers and watched television news programmes in large Northern Hemisphere countries that carried almost exclusively local news. The rest of the world either did not exist or it was irrelevant to their audience. This kind of parochialism is something that is far less widespread in New Zealand. Of course, there is parochialism, it is a universal human trait, but there seems to be less of it here. New Zealand cannot afford to concentrate entirely on itself.

Finally, our small size and isolation has produced something that has sometimes been called the 'cultural cringe'. Because we are so small and far away from the centres of power and 'culture', we lack the self-confidence to stand by what we have achieved and continually need to seek comment and approval from outsiders. We tend to play down our own achievements, but at the same time crave the praise and approval of outsiders. We continually ask other people's opinions of ourselves, but react badly if these opinions are not positive. So if you are asked what you think of New Zealand (and believe me, you will be asked that question a number of times), weigh your words carefully. Your Kiwi conversation partner is not looking for a considered judgement, he or she would like to hear you say how much you like this country. And let's face it: New Zealand is a country that is very easy to like.

THE BIRDS AND THE BEES

One of the many positive aspects of New Zealand is that it is virtually free of dangerous animals. There are no tigers or lions, snakes are unknown, and apart from a couple of varieties of poisonous spiders that prefer to scuttle for safety when a human approaches, the land has no animals or insects to be afraid of. If the tourist brochures describe New Zealand as 'paradise', it cannot be the Christian or Jewish Garden of Eden because that one contained the snake that tempted Eve. You will be completely safe from animals if you want to sleep out in the New Zealand bush.

The sea, however, is another matter. Sharks are sometimes known to attack an unwary swimmer and stingrays have injured people who accidentally trod on them, but such incidents are rare. Occasionally during summer, some swimming beaches are infested by a type of jellyfish that can cause unpleasant stings.

New Zealand is not only safe from animals that pose a threat to human life, it was a safe environment for birds as well, that is, before human settlement began. Apart from two species of harmless bats and the seals along its shores, it had no native mammals. All of them were introduced by human settlers, beginning with the *kiore*, the Polynesian rat that was brought along by the early Maori.

The original fauna of New Zealand consisted of birds. Foremost amongst them is the kiwi, a species of flightless birds that has become a New Zealand icon. Kiwis lost their ability to fly because of the absence of natural predators in the isolation of New Zealand. Kiwis, incidentally, are the only birds in the world that have nostrils at the end of their beaks, enabling them to smell out worms in the soil. Also saved by New Zealand's isolation is the *Tuatara*, a small reptile species that has survived here for many years unchanged since the time of the dinosaurs.

The Europeans settlers introduced mammals into New Zealand, and the story of their introduction reads very much like a version of *The Sorcerer's Apprentice*, in which the young lad who used his master's powers to get a bucket to fetch water from the public fountain, forgot the formula to stop the bucket and inadvertently flooded his master's house. Captain Cook had already brought pigs and goats to New Zealand. The 19th century settlers not only introduced domestic farm animals but also deer, pheasant, opossum, rats and even hedgehogs.

Rabbits were introduced and initially failed to thrive, particularly in the South Island. Once they took hold however, they soon became a pest because they multiplied, well, like rabbits. Farmers introduced stoats and weasels to try to control the rabbit population. The native birds would have helped control the rabbit population, but their habitat was severely reduced when large tracts of forests were cleared to make room for farmland. Furthermore, pests such as flies, fleas, cockroaches, earwigs, and other insects were introduced, by sheer carelessness, into the ecosystem and they multiplied rapidly, uncontrolled by the reduced bird population. In the 1860s, these insects became so numerous that a huge army of caterpillars crossing a railway line to attack a barley field actually stopped a train. The track was on an uphill grade, and the wheels of the locomotive lost traction on the rails. The cause of the slippery rails? Thousands of crushed caterpillars! The train managed to get going again by having sand on the tracks, but during the delay, many caterpillars had boarded the carriages and were thus carried to new parts of the country to further spread and multiply. One measure to attempt to control the insect population was the introduction of European birds, which today are part of New Zealand's bird population.

The New Zealand authorities are still working on containing the damage done by the indiscriminate introduction of foreign animals. Opossum and rabbit control cost millions of dollars. Offshore islands have been rid of goats and rats to allow the natural flora to regenerate and the indigenous birds to reestablish themselves. Deer are now farmed under controlled conditions, and a thriving industry has developed around them. There are now about two million deer being farmed on more than 4000 farms throughout the country. New Zealand is the major world supplier of venison today.

Fish

One of the success stories is the introduction of trout into New Zealand lakes and rivers. Brown trout was introduced from Tasmania, and Rainbow trout was brought in from California. To prevent poaching, free-run trout cannot be sold, so you will have to get your own gear and catch them yourself. The licences are inexpensive, and catching trout is as much fun as eating them. (Incidentally, while there are limits on the number of fish you can take, recreational fishing at sea does not require a licence in New Zealand).

FLORA

If the fauna is unique, so is the flora. Eighty percent of New Zealand's flora is unique to this country. The leaf of the giant tree fern has become one of the icons of New Zealand. The most impressive representative of the New Zealand forest is the majestic kauri. The tree has a long, straight trunk, branching out only near the top. The wood from the kauri tree was used for making masts and planks for ships. In the 19th century, forests were stripped of many kauri trees. The kauri is a slow growing tree and, while it is now protected, it will take a long time for them to reestablish themselves. The average kauri takes about 200 years to mature. The largest known kauri in New Zealand, *Tane Mahuta* (Lord of the Forest), has a circumference of over 13 m (43 feet) and an overall height of 51.5 m (169 feet). It is estimated that it is about 2100 years old.

New Zealand artists and artisans make small bowls and other small wooden utensils out of much older kauri wood called 'swamp' kauri. This refers to the timber from trees that were felled, possibly by volcanic activity, and then buried in peat swamps about 50,000 years ago. After the wood has been dried out—a delicate process that can take several years—it is made into attractive and unique souvenirs.

While the early Maori settlers brought with them yam and *kumara* (sweet potato) to supplement their diet of birds and seafood, the European colonists introduced many plant species to the land. For example, gorse, which is grown in Europe as a decorative hedge plant, has become a serious weed that has, for the past 100 years, taken over thousands of hectares of productive land. Gorse is also expensive to remove and control. Other introduced species, such as the European pine, *pinus radiata,* have proved more useful. The European pine trees have been planted to become huge forests, actively supplying a major New Zealand industry—timber.

Another import that is easily mistaken for a native New Zealand plant is the kiwifruit. This brown, fuzzy fruit with its bright green flesh and decorative star-shaped seeds is actually a native of China.

The seeds were brought to New Zealand in the early 20th century and planted in Wanganui in 1910. Horticulturists improved it over time, and it thrived in the volcanic soil of New Zealand. When I arrived in New Zealand, it was known as the Chinese gooseberry, and most home gardeners had a vine or two in their gardens. After all, they were tasty, decorative, and loaded with vitamin C. Although small quantities had been exported earlier, the 70s marked an upswing in exports, during which new varieties were developed. Kiwifruit soon became the darling of the New Zealand export fruit industry. It is now grown all over the world where the climate is right, but while I am, of course, totally unbiased, I still think that the New Zealand kiwifruit is by far the best.

BAH BAH BLACK SHEEP

In New Zealand, the largest export is dairy products, followed by meat and meat products.

A few years ago, I was travelling in Finland and had spent some hours on a train before arriving at my destination rather late. After I had settled into my hotel room, I went down to the restaurant for a late dinner and found to my delight that there was lamb on the menu. I ordered it and found that it was superbly well prepared. When the waitress came to clear away my plate, I told her that I had been very impressed with the lamb. She adopted a lecturing stance and informed me that the lamb meat had been imported from New Zealand. "That's where the best lamb in the world comes from, you know!" I told her how much I agreed with her and the next evening, ordered reindeer. After all, the best reindeer comes from Finland!

If we add the categories of wool, fruit and vegetables and other agricultural and seafood products, we find that primary produce makes up more than two-thirds of New Zealand's total exports. If this conjures up the picture of New Zealand as a giant farm, this is not too far from the truth, with half of the useable land in permanent pasture, and another one-quarter in forest and woodland. Nevertheless, an

Sheep graze on one of many farms found throughout New Zealand.

A milking shed on a dairy farm

astonishingly high proportion of the population (85%) lives in cities. What this tells us is that farming in New Zealand is very efficient, and it is not surprising that in many ways New Zealand farmers, with their ingenuity and Number-8-wire mentality, have led the world in the mechanisation of agriculture.

Today, the small farmer-owned dairy farms are beginning to give way to larger farms often owned by absentee owners who live in town. An employed manager and several workers operate these farms. In 1916, the traditional farming couple milked about 26 cows per day. The average New Zealand dairy herd size now is 251 cows, and larger farms are milking 500 cows per day.

But enough of animals. Perhaps we should take a bit of a closer look at the people that inhabit the islands of *Aotearoa/* New Zealand.

—*Chapter Two*—

THE PEOPLE

MAORI AND PAKEHA

Shortly after we were married, my Kiwi wife and I travelled to my native Switzerland and were, of course, invited to visit various relatives. One of the invitations included lunch with my great-grandaunt Lizzie. Shortly after we had arrived, Aunt Lizzie took me outside and, pointing to the front parlour where my wife was sitting, whispered to me, "but she looks just like one of us!" Not surprisingly, since my wife has Danish ancestors on her father's side, with Australian, Irish and even a bit of French on her mother's.

My great-grandaunt was very surprised because to her, who had never travelled far beyond her rural Swiss village, New Zealanders were brown-skinned people. And as we have seen in the last chapter, about 15% of the total population of New Zealand are indeed brown-skinned Maori, a Polynesian people who began to colonise these islands about a thousand years ago. The Polynesian migration to New Zealand did not stop altogether when the Europeans arrived. The third largest ethnic group in New Zealand, after the Europeans and the Maori, are the Pacific peoples who make up almost 6% of the population. The Maori and Pacific Island population in Auckland make this city the largest Polynesian city in the world.

While the *Pakeha* population is largely derived from British stock, there has also been significant immigration from the Netherlands, Yugoslavia, Germany and other European nations. Add that to an increasing number of immigrants from Asia, refugees from Indo-China and lesser numbers from places as far apart as Chile, Russia, Ethiopia, Bosnia and Somalia, and you arrive at the colourful and interesting mix that is New Zealand's population today.

Over the last two hundred years, the two major groups, Maori and *Pakeha*, have learned to live together. They have intermarried extensively and many of my Maori friends and acquaintances proudly point to the *Pakeha* ancestor or ancestors in their *whakapapa*. The *whakapapa* is an important aspect of Maori family tradition, and many Maori can recite them all the way back to the canoe in which their original ancestor travelled from Hawaiki to New Zealand. When I first arrived in New Zealand, I once travelled to Kawhia (on the west coast of the North Island) because I had been told that the last resting place of the *Tainui* canoe was behind the Maori meeting house on the foreshore of Kawhia Harbour. *Tainui* was one of the seven great *waka hourua* (voyaging canoes) that brought the first Maori settlers to New Zealand. The place where it is buried is marked by two stones and fenced in because it is sacred ground. As I stood there, contemplating what was obviously a very important site, an old man came up to me and gave me some of the history including the genealogical links that bound him to that canoe. I was far too young and far too unfamiliar with Maori culture to appreciate the honour done to me.

One of the fundamental differences between Maori and *Pakeha* culture is enshrined in the concept of *mana*, which is perhaps best, though inadequately, translated as 'renown' or 'prestige'. This derives, to a large extent, from the person's lineage and is part of the reason why the *whakapapa* is so important to a Maori. At the same time, a person's *mana* can be earned and must be maintained and enhanced through active participation in the life of the *marae* (Maori meeting grounds).

In many European societies, a person's social standing is determined by their profession or, perhaps, even more important, by their wealth. Not so in Maori society. Lineage and family connections are far more important. People new to New Zealand, and even *Pakeha*, are often surprised when the *kaumatua* (elder) who presides at a Maori function is by no means someone who would be regarded as having high social standing in *Pakeha* society. A few years ago, when the body of a Maori friend of mine was lying in a special room in the hospital where he had died, waiting for collection by his people, the senior members of Maoridom who attended to him and the mourners who were gathering were not the Maori doctors, but some of the cleaners and orderlies. These people outranked their Maori colleagues who, by the *Pakeha* system, would have seemed more important. It is therefore important for new arrivals in New Zealand, and for New Zealanders, to be aware that two cultures also means two social systems, and to make sure that they are sensitive to this when dealing with Maori, either socially or professionally.

After some vigorous Maori protests and land occupations in the 1970s culminating in a land march to the New Zealand parliament, the injustices of the earlier colonial period are now gradually being addressed. The Waitangi Tribunal, an advisory body to the New Zealand government, is investigating each Maori tribe's claims (often well founded) of illegal alienation of land by the then government, and is recommending what action can be taken to compensate the tribes for their loss. This is, of course, a huge task. Some of the records are either deliberately or accidentally vague. There is often a discrepancy between the tribal history and the 'official' *Pakeha* version, and at times, there is conflict within the tribe about who should represent it before the commission. Because the task is so enormous, it usually takes a long time. Nevertheless, progress is being made, and each successful settlement aids in settling another grievance. One of the problems with the Treaty of Waitangi is that it was written in English and then translated into Maori by an English missionary who may not have been conversant with all the subtleties of the Maori language. There still are ongoing discussions about the precise meaning of some of the terms used.

For race-related grievances today, there is the government-appointed Race Relations Conciliator whose office is charged with investigating any complaint of racism or discrimination. Given the racial mix in the New Zealand population, the complaints are by no means only relating to *Pakeha* exploitation of non-Europeans. In 2000, a Thai couple was convicted of running a sweatshop with illegal Thai labourers in a suburb of Auckland.

I believe that there is less overt racism in New Zealand compared with most other multiracial countries. Some of my international students however, have told me that they have encountered some instances of covert racism, such as racist comments. But most of the students affected in this way either shrug it off or, if it persists, ask for help informally by informing someone in authority. On the whole, New Zealanders are easy-going people, and at times what may seem like a racial issue is resolved with a bit of give and take. My middle son worked for a time in the fines office of the local court. One day, a young Maori came in to pay an instalment of his fine, obviously not very happy about having to part with his hard-earned cash. When my son asked him how his name was spelled, the Maori started to heap abuse on him for being a racist *Pakeha* who did not even know how to spell Maori names. My son listened for a while and then quietly asked the enraged customer whether he would care to attempt spelling my son's name. When the client heard the name, he had to admit that he was stumped, and the tension dissolved in mutual laughter.

Sometimes racism is read into a situation that is simply misbehaviour. A young rascal recently took to throwing lemons at houses in our neighbourhood, and our Chinese neighbours were convinced their house had been selected as a target because they were newly-arrived Chinese. We had some difficulty in convincing them that this was not the case; that our houses had also received the same unwelcome attention by the rascal.

As in other countries, opportunist politicians in New Zealand have tried to use racism in an attempt to get votes. Because of the multi-cultural makeup of New Zealand's population, there is usually a fairly quick negative reaction.

One of the effects of the two peoples living together has been on the English spoken in New Zealand. The Maori *kia ora* (hello) is now a fairly common greeting, even though not so long ago there was an uproar in the press when a Maori telephone operator regularly used it to greet customers. But there are many more words that have made the transition from Maori into New Zealand English and are commonly understood. This may be a bit confusing at first, but you will soon learn that when a Maori speaker tells you that the whole *whanau* turned up for the *hui* on the *marae*, it means that the whole extended family turned up for the meeting at the square in front of the Maori meeting house, the *whare nui*. If they have to attend a *tangi*, they are going to a funeral. If an advertisement for a concert or other event has the note 'Admission by *koha*', it means that there is no fixed admission price, and you are invited to make a donation instead. In most cases, these words will not be translated. They have become part of New Zealand English and give it its distinctive character.

Maori appreciate it if you pronounce their language properly. The first thing you have to remember is that, unlike English, Maori uses phonetic spelling, which means that every letter represents a single sound. However, Maori does not have as many letters as English; there is no *s*, for example, and no *y*. This means that the Maori version of 'Sydney', is, in fact, 'Hirini'. The second basic principle is that in

Maori words, every syllable is pronounced, and every syllable ends in a vowel. The vowels are pronounced as they would be in Latin or in German:

A (long) as in 'dark'
A (short) as in 'cup'
E (long) as in 'bread'
E (short) as in 'let'
I (long) as in 'feed'
I (short) as in 'bit'
O (long) as in 'pork'
O (short) as in 'port'
U (long) as in 'moon'
U (short) as in 'put'

The only two consonants that are a bit different are *wh*, which is pronounced like a voiced *f*, and *ng* which is pronounced like the *ng* sound in 'singer'. As you can see from the table, vowels in Maori can be short or long. If they are long, they are sometimes written as double vowels, or else they may have a little macron sign (-) over them.

While I cannot give you a full course in the pronunciation of Maori, the best way to tackle a Maori word is to divide it up into its syllables and then pronounce it syllable by syllable. Thus, the small town on the main railway line between Auckland and Wellington, Taumarunui, would be pronounced, tow-ma-roo-nui, with all syllables roughly equally stressed. As a newcomer, you may make mistakes, and I suggest you ask if you are unsure about how to pronounce a word. Sadly, the early English-speaking settlers actively discouraged the use of the Maori language and it was almost lost. Only in 1997 was Maori made an official language of New Zealand. Efforts are now being made to encourage Maori to become fluent speakers again. For example, in 1996, the first Maori-owned Maori language radio station, Ruia Mai, began operating. More recently in 2003, the government-funded Maori Television Service was launched. One of its aims is to broadcast at least half of its prime-time programmes in

Maori by the middle of 2004. All radio and TV presenters and all government employees are now given instruction in the correct pronunciation of Maori. After all, it is one of the *taonga* (treasures) of the Maori people and deserves to be treated with respect.

It would be naive to claim that New Zealand has achieved its goal of total racial equality and harmony. Maori are still under-represented in the professions, and they are sadly over-represented in the lower socio-economic groups and in the prison population. There is still a long way to go, but progress is being made. Government initiatives also assist with solving problems along the way.

One of the associated issues is what has become known as political correctness. It is a term that is applied to people who make sure, for example, that their language is always gender and race inclusive. Unfortunately, the term has taken on overtones of ridicule and some journalists, for example, apply the word to people who overdo it. I recently heard the broadcast of a church service from one of the city churches. A woman was reading a verse from the New Testament. I have forgotten the exact passage, but it was about one of the apostles, obviously a man. Nevertheless, the reader replaced every 'he' with 'he or she'. This may have been politically correct but it was certainly biologically incorrect. I personally have no problem with using inclusive language and respecting people's views even if they are not my own, neither do most New Zealanders, as far as I can tell. The problem is with people that overdo it. I am perfectly happy if in a Maori setting a *karakia* (prayer) is offered before a meal or a meeting. This is their way and I respect that. However, if some politically correct *Pakeha* tries to do the same in a *Pakeha* setting with no Maori present, I consider that to be inappropriate.

CITY AND COUNTRY

With agricultural and horticultural products among the major exports of New Zealand, you would expect that the majority of the population lives off the land. Indeed, one of the New Zealand stereotypes is the down-to-earth farmer who stomps around his property in black rubber boots, called *gumboots* in New Zealand, shorts, and a black woollen singlet, attended by his faithful sheep or cattle dogs. While there are indeed such farmers, 85% of New Zealanders live in urban areas. But again, 'urban' means something slightly different from what it would mean, for example, in Asia or the United States. I recently travelled to India and Indonesia. In the three weeks of my trip, I visited quite a number of cities, and only one of them had a smaller population than the entire population of New Zealand. Auckland, New Zealand's largest urban area, has a population of about 1.2 million.

In spite of the fact that most New Zealanders live in cities, most of them have some connection to the land, even if it is only a basic knowledge of the various types of farming that goes on around them. Most Kiwis will be able to list a few sheep and cattle breeds, and many will be able to explain what that sinister-looking machine does in that field over there. The caricature of the city dweller who thinks that milk comes out of a carton does not really apply here. I know of some visiting American students from one of the major cities in the United States who had hysterics when they discovered that chickens actually had necks and heads. I am quite proud of the fact that when I was a young lecturer at the university, I occasionally went to help out my farmer father. It meant that before I got to the university to take a seminar on medieval German literature, I would have milked some 150 cows!

Their small size does not mean that New Zealand cities are totally neglected provincial backwaters. In the larger ones, there is now a lively restaurant and bar scene, and even some of the smaller ones, like Rotorua and Queenstown, for example, have an entertainment infrastructure because they are centres of tourism. The development of a comparatively sophisticated city environment is quite recent. I still remember the time, a few decades ago, when Auckland had a total of four restaurants licensed to sell alcohol with their meals, and the scandal when the first licensed restaurant in Hamilton was closed down after some medical students had discovered that the bones of the 'chicken' they were eating were, in fact, cat bones!

Living in the city, most New Zealanders have a bit of 'country' all the same. The great majority of Kiwis (71%) own a single-family home with a bit of garden around it. This means that New Zealand cities and towns occupy more land than cities in many other countries where a large proportion of the urban population lives in high-density housing. New Zealand's largest city Auckland, for example, spreads its population of 1.2 million over more than a thousand square kilometres. Gardens, parks, schools with generous green playing fields, sports venues and even full 18-hole golf courses are part of the New Zealand cityscape. They contribute to an environment that allows the urban population of New Zealand to enjoy what in many countries would be a semi-rural lifestyle, while still having access to the amenities of a city.

Let us return to the black-singleted, gumbooted farmer striding or riding on horseback across his kingdom with his faithful dogs. Although people living in the country make up only 15% of the

population, as we have seen, and they are not all farmers, they produce well over half the total export income for the country. This is because all through the last century, New Zealand country folk, particularly farmers, have led the world in the mechanization of pastoral farming. The advent and constant improvement of milking machines and mechanical shearing meant that a single farming couple or family could manage larger and larger herds of sheep and cattle.

The typical farmer of today still covers a lot of ground over his or her property and yes, gumboots and black singlets are still worn by real life farmers and don't only appear in cartoons. One enterprising central North Island town, Taihape, has even introduced an annual gumboot throwing contest, complete with rules and champions!

Today, however, the trusty horse has, in many cases, been replaced by the three-or four-wheeled farm bike with fat knobbly tires and a tray on the back where the dog rides in comfort on the way to and from work. Tractors have also been modernised. I well remember driving my father's tractor when feeding hay to the cows in winter, being lashed by driving rain which inevitably found its way inside my collar and ran down my body in icy rivulets. At a recent major agricultural exhibition, tractors with the latest safety roll cages and enclosed cabs that could be heated or air conditioned were shown and found eager buyers.

It is, however, the old fashioned farmer that has become an icon in New Zealand. John Clarke, a New Zealand humorist who created the archetypal farmer character called Fred Dagg, has written a song, which became very popular, entirely in praise of gumboots. Here is an excerpt:

Whenever I sing at the opera, my gumboots are a must.
They help me hit the high notes, and protect me feet from dust.
They keep the water well away, so me voice won't get no rust.
You will not never see me without me gumboots.

And the refrain goes:

If it weren't for your gumboots, where would ya be?
You'd be in the hospital or infirmary
'coz you would have a dose of the 'flu, or even pleurisy
If ya didn't have yer feet in yer gumboots.

I always find it a bit ironic that one of my very few trips to the Accident and Emergency department at our local hospital was due precisely to the fact that I was wearing gumboots. I was washing down the milking shed after morning milking when I slipped on some wooden steps while carrying a bucket of boiling water. The water slopped into my gumboots and caused quite severe burns. If I had not been wearing them, the injuries would have been less severe!

Unlike farming settlements in many parts of the world, New Zealand country villages are not inhabited by farmers, but by the local service providers, the shopkeeper, the garage mechanic, the schoolteacher, the clergyman. The farmers themselves live on their properties, and if they are on large sheep farms, they are often many kilometres away from their nearest neighbour. Some sheep farmer friends of ours have a drive of several kilometres just to get to their letterbox, and the nearest town of any size is over an hour's drive away. Like many farmers, particularly those in remote locations, they are quite self-sufficient. They have their own water supply, kill their own meat, have a house cow in the paddock near the house for milk, as well as a vegetable garden and a small fruit orchard. A happy flock of free range hens provide eggs, and the wife can make her own butter and bread.

While the life of a Kiwi farmer may sound idyllic, and there are certainly many positive aspects to it, there are also some drawbacks. The remote location of many farms means that an evening in town for a show or a visit to the cinema is a major expedition from which they may not return until well after midnight. If there is an accident or a medical emergency, help is just that much further away, although some base hospitals now have helicopter links for urgent cases. And getting away for a holiday is also much harder, particularly in single family units where a relief worker has to be arranged to look after the livestock and attend to the many small tasks a farmer has to carry out daily. Farmers' children also have to make some sacrifices. While there is usually a good school bus service, the length of some of the runs makes it impossible for the children to attend any after-school sports activities because the bus leaves as soon as the last teaching period is over. Larger regional towns usually have a secondary school with Monday to Friday boarding facilities to allow the country pupils to enjoy more educational opportunities, but that means, of course, that the children can no longer live at home during the week.

Because of its comparative isolation, the farming community often is a very close-knit community. When we first arrived in New Zealand, it was just hay-making time, and my father—at the time a very inexperienced farmer—set out to mow the first paddock. As he was driving his tractor with the mower attached, he noticed another tractor with a mower approaching. The driver was a neighbour from down the road with whom we had talked for a total of perhaps ten minutes when he and his wife had come over to our house to welcome us. He waved to my father, lowered his mower and simply joined in. Nobody had asked him to come, indeed we had not even told anyone that we were cutting grass for hay on that day. He had simply seen my father make a start and decided to come over and help.

New Zealand's farmers have often been described as the backbone of the country, and they certainly have an important position in the country's economic and social makeup. In many countries, farmers are seen as peasants, with a comparatively low social standing. This certainly is not the case in New Zealand. Several famous New Zealand prime ministers were farmers before being elected to parliament. One of them, William Massey, the story goes, was handed the telegram informing him that he had won the election on the end

A farmer uses a farm vehicle to move about his land.

of a pitchfork while he was building a haystack. Today, many young farmers, despite the fact that they have grown up on a farm, will have the benefit of a university degree. Two universities in particular, Massey University (Palmerston North) and Lincoln University (just outside Christchurch), offer degrees in various aspects of agriculture.

There is also a popular national competition called the 'Young Farmer of the Year'. The participants compete in a number of practical tasks required for the running of a modern farm. They also have to demonstrate their ability to develop a farm into a financially viable business. In addition, they also get tested on their general knowledge. All in all, a pretty gruelling test, you'll agree. The competition is broadcast on national television in prime time where it draws a large audience not only from country dwellers, but from town people as well. Another popular TV programme that features New Zealand farming is a series called *Country Calendar*.

Most of the Kiwi farmers are proud of their calling and enjoy the lifestyle. And there certainly must be something to it, because an increasing number of 'townies' buy small farmlets on the outskirts of towns and cities, where they live and run a few head of cattle or sheep or graze a few horses. Perhaps, they enjoy the best of both worlds— the luxury of having a few hectares of land and your own animals, as well as the proximity of a larger centre of population with all its amenities.

YOUNG AND OLD

New Zealand has an aging population. It is a result of sharply falling fertility and increased life expectancy. Add to that the fact that the baby boom children are now approaching middle age and retirement, and you can understand why the government is worried about being able to provide financially for an increasing number of retired people with the tax it collects from a decreasing pool of people in full-time employment. The solution they have come up with is to put aside a considerable amount of money over the next few years and invest it. The proceeds will then be used to top up pensions for the retired and elderly.

New Zealand has often been praised as a good country in which to bring up children. Having brought up our children mostly in New Zealand, with a couple of years in other countries while I was on sabbatical leave from the university, I would agree with this. It is, by world standards, comparatively safe. It has wonderful beaches, rivers and mountains; there is plenty of space, easy access to nature, and many amenities to foster the development of healthy bodies. It has a progressive school system, which will be examined in some detail later, and above all, New Zealand is a children-friendly country.

I still remember one of our sabbaticals in Europe. We were on holiday with our three children who at the time were aged four, six and eight. One day, we came to a beautiful lake just in time to have lunch and discovered a delightful park at the lake's edge. What a place for a picnic! We piled out of the car and the children, relieved to be set free from the confined space, happily ran towards the lake. We followed at a more sedate pace until we saw a sign prominently placed between the parking area and the inviting wooden seats at the shore. 'Children and dogs are to be kept under control at all times.'

I have never seen such a sign in New Zealand. If there is a problem with children running wild in a shop, for example, the shopkeeper might try some humour, like the one in a tourist shop not far from where I live. She had obviously had goods damaged or spoiled by unsupervised children. So she hung a sign on the wall. It read: 'Children caught damaging goods will be sold for medical experiments.'

Overall however, Kiwi parents are fairly easy-going with their children and, as a result, Kiwi children are a fairly relaxed bunch. They are happiest being barefooted, dressed in casual clothes and being allowed to run on the grass. The only problem is that as a proportion of the overall population, there just aren't as many of them as there used to be.

Probably as a result of their upbringing, New Zealand young people are quite open about themselves. A clinical psychologist who had immigrated to New Zealand and who works with young people told me that in his view, young people in New Zealand were much more up front and 'in your face' about the things young people do, such as drinking alcohol. He considered that young people will be young people anywhere in the world, but that in many societies, behaviour that is frowned upon by the elders is covered up. The 'bad' behaviour is still there, but not acknowledged. Young Kiwis generally have no problems with telling you what they are up to. You may not like it, particularly if you are their parent, but at least you will have some idea about what they are doing.

Related to this trait is what many cultures would regard as a lack of respect for authority figures. Some years ago, I visited a university in Thailand on Teachers' Day. While I was talking to one of the professors, a young student knocked on the door and when she had been given permission, she came into the room. She then knelt on the floor in front of the professor, confessed that she had not been diligent enough in her studies and promised to do better in the next term. With this, she presented him with a garland of flowers. When I told this story to my class back here in New Zealand, they roared with laughter. It was simply unthinkable for them that a Kiwi kid would do the same to his or her teacher. So if you come from a culture where children, in the good old Victorian phrase, are 'seen but not heard', do not expect the same in New Zealand. At the same time, try not to take offence at what you may see as a lack of respect.

There are, as we have seen, increasing numbers of elderly Kiwis, and they generally have different needs from the young, but the availability and relative affordability of sports such as golf and bowls keeps them active. I have an acquaintance who is now in his seventies. He lives in Auckland, not far from a beach, and he goes swimming every morning, virtually all the year round. Most of the social amenities for seniors that one would expect in a developed country are available. They include special exercise classes, lecture series, outings. There is even something called the SeniorNet, an organisation consisting of learning centres where seniors go to learn more about computers. There, they not only have access to computers but also staff who can assist them if the newfangled technology gets too much for them.

In this context, I read recently of a lovely initiative to bring together old and young. A school had decided to open its computer laboratory once a week for elderly people. They also provided the tutors: schoolchildren who had just acquired their computer skills and were eager to pass them on. So here was a reversal of roles; the young were teaching their grandmothers and grandfathers, and both instructors and students were enjoying every minute of it. The teacher who had initiated the scheme commented that it also helped the young people to learn social skills from older people.

People who are too old to look after themselves have access to a whole range of services to assist them staying in their own home if that is what they would like to do. The 'Meals on Wheels' programme, which delivers cooked food to the elderly, is staffed by volunteer drivers. Home help is also available through various agencies, and alterations can be made to homes to make living in them easier for elderly people. Of course, there are rest homes for old people who prefer to live in a community or who need constant medical care. The options range from small apartments with or without meal plans, to a room in the geriatric hospital section of the home.

RELIGION

When the British Queen (who is also queen of New Zealand) visited New Zealand in 2002, she was entertained to a state dinner by our prime minister. The prime minister caused quite a stir in the press because she did not have a senior clergyman say grace before the meal. When questioned about it, she pointed out that New Zealand was now a secular country and saying grace was no longer relevant, at least, in her view. Many writers of letters to the editor of the daily papers begged to differ.

In many ways, she is right. The number of New Zealanders who describe themselves as Christian is declining, and many will attend church only for celebrations like Christmas and Easter, if at all. Anglicans (or Church of England) are by far the largest single Christian denomination in New Zealand, making up about 18% of the population, followed by Roman Catholics and Presbyterians.

With recent migration patterns, there has been an increase in non-Christian religions, with Buddhists and Muslims more than doubling their numbers between 1991 and 1996, while the number of Hindus increased by more than half. Admittedly, each of these religions accounts for less than 1% of the total population.

Although the largest proportion of New Zealanders profess a religion, the prime minister's statement that New Zealand is a secular

A small mosque is the venue for Muslims doing their Friday prayers.

state is correct. The state schools do not provide religious instruction unless they are former church schools that are now funded by the state. It is the churches and other religious institutions that teach their young the tenets of their faith.

Religious freedom is one of the basic rights of New Zealanders, and you will find that most major religions (and some very minor ones as well) are catered for. Within a short drive from my home, there is a mosque, a Sikh temple, a Mormon temple and numerous churches. There is even a *halal* butcher not far away. If you are looking for a particular religious community in the place where you live, the Citizens Advice Bureau, described in detail later, will be able to help.

If you are a Christian, many of the mainstream denominations that I have listed before have also established ethnic sub-congregations with their own priests and ministers. So you can attend the Korean Presbyterian service or the Mandarin Baptist service and countless others in most larger New Zealand towns and cities.

The fact that New Zealand is an increasingly secular society does not mean that the Christian religion does not have a role to play. The New Zealand parliament, for example, is still opened daily with a Christian prayer, and many of New Zealand's laws are based on Christian principles, particularly its social legislation. It is interesting to note that the colonist descendants of the Christian missionaries have largely turned away from practising their faith, while the Maori whom they came to convert have a much stronger tradition of adhering to Christian rituals. As we will see later in this book, every formal meal in a Maori setting is prefaced with a *karakia*, a prayer giving thanks for the food. Also every Maori business meeting that I have attended did not get under way until one of the senior men had spoken a prayer.

At the same time, many Maori have integrated their Christian beliefs and practices into their pre-Christian theology. Quite recently, the government was planning to modernise and upgrade the major road that runs between Auckland and Hamilton. At one point, the road comes close to the Waikato River. When the plans were announced, the local Maori people made the point that the new road alignment would interfere with the lair of a *taniwha*, a water sprite. As a result of discussion, a solution was found. The road will now be a bit dearer to build than the original plan, but the home of the *taniwha* will remain undisturbed.

PUBLIC BEHAVIOUR

On the whole, New Zealanders are very orderly people. Unless they have had a bit too much to drink, they will avoid being boisterous or rowdy in public, and locals or foreigners who are will be frowned upon. Kiwis are generally not very demonstrative in public, and hugs between males or backslapping are rarely seen. The sports ground is the exception to this rule. Any sports game, especially by a national team, will be attended by a very demonstrative and passionate crowd of Kiwis. But even there, New Zealanders seem to be more restrained than sports fans in other cultures. For example, we do not have the football hooligans that plague sports venues in other countries, although there are isolated incidents occasionally.

New Zealanders also tend to avoid any show of ostentation. There are a few stretch limos in the country now, but these would be used mainly for weddings and, of course, foreign tourists. In 2000, a newspaper article in the *New Zealand Herald* reported that most of our cabinet ministers, who are entitled to cars at taxpayers' expense, drive relatively modest cars. The Prime Minister herself was then said to be driving an 18-month-old Mitsubishi.

The practical application of this for expatriates is quite simple. If you have a lot of money or prestige (or both!), don't flaunt it in public. Your New Zealand friends and neighbours will certainly not appreciate it, and it will make it more difficult for you to 'fit in'.

Queuing

A particular convention that New Zealand shares with a number of other cultures is queuing. At bus stops, cinema ticket counters, supermarket checkouts, in banks, offices, wherever a number of people have to be attended to, New Zealanders will form a queue. Never become a 'queue jumper', i.e. somebody that will force his way into a queue or go to the front, unless there is a very important reason why you should do so (which you will have to explain to the people you pass). New Zealand so far has very few of the machines you see in other countries, where you get a ticket with a number on it and then go to the booth or counter when your number shows. People are simply too orderly and polite to jump a queue. Unless you want to become the focus of odium and contempt, you will respect orderly queuing. I once even saw a fight at a taxi stand when one waiting customer thought the other was trying to jump the queue. Admittedly, the taxi stand was outside a hotel and one or both of them had had a bit too much to drink.

Smiling

After my experiences in many large cities around the world, I am always struck by the fact that New Zealanders tend to smile a lot in public – at perfect strangers! You step back and let someone enter the supermarket first, and they will smile to thank you. The supermarket checkout operator will greet you and often smile when it is your turn to have your groceries processed. You drive a car and stop at a pedestrian crossing for some waiting person, and chances are, the person crossing will smile at you and wave a little thanks. Don't be afraid to respond to these friendly gestures. It costs nothing and gives a little pleasure to both parties.

Greetings

Just as in other English-speaking countries, Kiwis will often greet you by asking 'how are you'. This is a polite phrase and does not require a full answer about your mental and physical condition. The most common response is 'fine, thank you', even if you are not feeling particularly well. I remember greeting a colleague in the lift with this question and he answered " You don't really want to know". When I told him that I did genuinely want to know, he promptly burst into a flood of tears, so I took him to my office and listened to his troubles for half an hour. In normal circumstances however, 'how are you' is simply an extension of a greeting such as 'hello'.

Attire

In their 'off' time when Kiwis are not working—and possibly having to adhere to a dress code (more about that under Business)—New Zealanders dress informally. Even on some semiformal occasions, they may not dress up to avoid a misunderstanding. Quite some years ago now, a student visited one of my colleagues who was a German university professor. It was in the middle of summer and the student arrived wearing shorts, a short sleeved shirt, and NO SHOES! I

47

witnessed the meeting through his open door. My colleague drew himself up to his full height and barked at the astonished student to come back once he was dressed fit to see a professor!

Not wearing shoes and socks is quite acceptable in a range of situations where it would not be in other countries. I recently watched the shopping crowd on the footpath of a small country town during a Saturday morning one summer. It was a beautiful sunny day, and the shops were doing a brisk trade. In the space of ten minutes, I counted four shoppers, all of them in their early twenties, who were not wearing shoes. I'm sure nobody else took particular notice. I personally tend to wear at least sandals, but around the house I also prefer not to wear any footwear when it is warm. If you visit a New Zealand home unannounced, and the person you are visiting comes to the door barefooted, don't take it as a sign of disrespect or rudeness. Many newcomers to New Zealand interpret the free and easy behaviour (such as not wearing shoes) as a lack of manners or a lack of money, as my colleague did. An elderly lady who had recently arrived in New Zealand made the observation that New Zealanders generally lacked manners. It is true that 'manners' relate to social ritual, and more formal societies require a greater degree of ritual. I often have to try not to take offence at what I see as the lack of 'manners' in our young people. But there are always two sides to the coin. I remember a few years back watching two ladies dressed in traditional kimono taking leave from each other late one evening in a subway station in Osaka. Their mutual bowing went on and on and on. I was quite touched by the scene because here were two people who had obviously enjoyed an evening together expressing, within their social ritual, their pleasure and thanks for the company of the other. You would never see this in New Zealand, but New Zealanders have their own, very informal way, of expressing the same emotions. They may not have 'manners' if you expect them to conform to certain set patterns of social behaviour, but most of them are friendly, warm and respectful towards you, expecting the same in return.

I have already mentioned that New Zealand is a secular country, and this is also reflected in the New Zealand street scene. You rarely see priests and ministers of religion dressed in the traditional clerical garb apart from the odd nun in a (usually modernised) habit or the rare Buddhist monk. Clothing denoting religious vocation has disappeared from the New Zealand city streets. So be careful; that man wearing rings on his fingers and sporting tattoos and dreadlocks may turn out to be a priest.

Also absent from New Zealand streets (with the possible exception of the capital, Wellington) are vehicles displaying special signs and lights and claiming the right of way because they are carrying government officials. This again is part of New Zealand's egalitarianism. Government officials, no matter how high, drive ordinary cars and are subject to the same traffic rules as the rest of us. One morning, I walked in a Wellington street near the House of Parliament. Suddenly, a well-known cabinet minister appeared from a side road. He was wearing sports gear and had obviously just been for his morning run. He disappeared into the building. No doubt he had a shower and a change of clothes available in there. No doubt, he also had an official car and driver available for official business. But this is New Zealand and everything is low-key.

Another aspect of the street scene that may be unfamiliar to people from outside New Zealand is the comparative frequent use of tattoos, particularly among the Polynesian population. Tattooing is an ancient Polynesian custom. The Christian missionaries of the 19th century frowned on it as a heathen practice. With the Maori cultural renaissance however, it has become increasingly popular over the last couple of decades. So do not be surprised if, from time to time, you encounter a Maori who has a full facial tattoo, a *moko*, or a Samoan whose legs are fully tattooed.

About 30 years ago, New Zealand was a country where a large proportion of the population smoked tobacco, and smoking was generally accepted. I even remember a small airline set up in competition with the domestic air services of Air New Zealand. The one (and only) time I flew with them, the attendant came down the aisle and distributed free cigarettes as soon as the captain had switched off the No Smoking sign.

This has changed over the last 25 years. In 1990, the government enacted the Smoke-free Environments Act which makes provision for smoke-free workplaces, non-smoking sections in restaurants and bars (at least half of each restaurant must be reserved for non-smokers), and prohibits smoking in aircraft and buses, public waiting rooms, and indoor queuing areas. Trains and ferries are generally smoke-free, unless there is a designated area for smokers. The Act also makes it illegal for shopkeepers to sell tobacco products to anyone under 16, and this is strictly controlled. A few weeks back, I was standing in a supermarket checkout queue. The young man in front of me asked for a packet of cigarettes. When the checkout operator asked him for evidence that he was 16, he mumbled, 'Forget it', and left without having made his purchase.

As a result of the legislation and also of social pressure, smoking is gradually declining in New Zealand. At the moment, about 25% of New Zealanders smoke, and special efforts are being made to target the group that has the largest proportion of smokers: Maori, particularly young Maori women.

OCCASIONS AND CELEBRATIONS

Many countries in the world have established festivals and celebrations that go back into the mists of time. The people who observe them sometimes are not aware of the origins and the true significance of the spring rituals, harvest celebrations or winter and summer solstice romps that mark the passing of significant and recurring milestones in the year.

New Zealand is a young country and its two principal settler groups, Maori and *Pakeha*, brought some of the traditions of their home societies with them and transplanted them into this new

A carved maori meeting house is the venue of many Maori celebrations.

environment. One of the important Polynesian customs that is still observed by the Maori population is that if guests are invited to an occasion, be it a wedding, a funeral, a meeting, they must be given something to eat. We hear tales of enormous *hakari* (feasts) in the old days. I have read the description of such a feast in the papers of a German missionary who worked in New Zealand in the mid-19th century. He reports that when he arrived in Taranaki on the west coast of the North Island, the local Maori tribe arranged a *hakari* to welcome him. Preparations were made long before the feast was held; extra food was grown and larger numbers of fish were caught and dried. When the feast was held, the estimated 3.6 tons of fish were displayed on a scaffold 1.5 m (5 feet) high and approximately 20 m (67 feet) long. Two thousand baskets of vegetables and other food were arranged along the scaffold, and the missionary estimates that between 26 and 27 tons of food were consumed at the feast which lasted several days. Being a missionary, the reporter of this feast emphasized the religious observances in his description that he sent back to his superiors. This was to make sure that they would not think that he and his flock had succumbed to the sin of gluttony!

Feasts on that scale are no longer held, but I have been to some associated with weddings, funerals or our university's graduation ceremonies which sometimes take place in the tribal areas from which the Maori graduates come. They are held on the *marae*, the Maori gathering place or village square which is dominated by the *whare nui*, the large meeting house, although the *kai* (food) is always served in a separate building. The hospitality is always very warm and generous, and the food, which is explained in a later chapter, is always delicious and plentiful. To make sure that the host tribe or extended family do not have to bear the entire cost of entertaining the guests alone, the visitors, who normally arrive in groups, hand over a contribution or *koha* (gift), which is presented at the formal *powhiri* (welcome).

If you ever get an invitation to attend a Maori celebration on a *marae*, I would strongly urge you to accept if at all possible. You will need to set aside plenty of time. I have been to some where the *powhiri* alone took well over three hours. But it is here that you can experience the richness of Maori culture. You can attend an abbreviated welcome for tourists in Rotorua, but if you are invited, and you may well be if you work with Maori or for a government department, don't miss the real thing.

While every tribe has its own protocol for the welcoming ceremony, you normally gather with the group that has been invited outside the *marae* at the appointed time. Sometimes, you may have to wait a little while the senior men of the hosts and guest groups sort out the protocol, but eventually you will be called onto the *marae* by the *karanga*, the call of one or several senior women of the tribe. You advance slowly and are directed to some benches in front of the meeting house, facing another lot of benches across the square where your hosts are sitting. If you are not sure where to sit, just stay with your group and allow one of the Maori in your group to direct you. In some tribes, the men sit in the front rows of seats, with the most senior in the first row, while the women have to sit at the back. The explanation I have been given for this is that in the old days, if a fight broke out between the guests and the hosts before the welcome had been completed, the men would be in front to ensure that their womenfolk were protected.

When all are seated, the speeches begin. They are in Maori and can be quite long. If you are lucky, you may have a Maori speaker beside you who can provide a translation. If not, just enjoy the experience. You will know when the speech is over because the speaker will be joined by his group for a *waiata*, a song, chant, or dance. Maori around you may stand and join in the *waiata*, but it is fine if you remain seated.

When the speeches are all over, and as I warned you, they can take several hours, the hosts will form a long line and you join a queue of the guests who will then pass along the assembled hosts for the *hongi*, the pressing of noses. You touch the nose of each of your hosts with your nose, normally twice. Just take your cue from the person who is greeting you. The *hongi* is just like shaking hands or bowing in other cultures. It is a formal acknowledgement of the meeting of two persons. I have found that complications can arise if you are both wearing glasses or academic headdress. It means that more than just your noses meet in a (hopefully) controlled collision.

Once the *hongi* is over, you are a guest of the local people and I can assure you that you will be warmly hosted. Whatever the occasion, it will be an unforgettable experience. A hallmark of the Maori culture is their hospitality. Measured time means nothing; the most important thing is that a visitor feels welcomed.

Because Maori society was and still is very much concentrated on the extended family and the tribe, all Maori celebrations are connected with family and tribal events. There are comparatively few nationwide festivals and occasions, and those that have developed are of recent origin and are influenced by European usage. The anniversary of the coronation of the Maori queen is celebrated with events centred on her official residence in Ngaruawahia, just north of Hamilton. Another Maori celebration that normally attracts nationwide coverage is the birthday of Tahupotiki Wiremu Ratana in January. Ratana was a Maori prophet, faith healer and campaigner who founded his own church, the Ratana church, in 1918. He also led a political movement. His birthday is celebrated annually on his farm at Ratana *pa* (settlement), near Marton. Like the Ratana religion, the festival consists of an amalgam of traditional Maori and European elements. Maori warriors in traditional dress alternate with uniformed brass bands. These celebrations are attended by senior politicians and are often accorded national television coverage.

Christmas

The festivals and traditions introduced by *Pakeha* into New Zealand culture, although predominantly British, come from many sources. Their common denominator is perhaps the Christian religion, with Christmas and Easter as the two most prominent festivals.

The problem here in New Zealand is that Christmas, a traditional winter festival, falls in midsummer in the Southern Hemisphere. This means that many Kiwis celebrate this festival at the beach, because Christmas also coincides with the long summer holiday. Another popular pattern is to have Christmas at home and then depart for the summer break.

Wherever we are for Christmas however, the European imagery is still there. Shop windows are decorated with cotton wool snow, while Santa Clauses pose in front of cardboard sleighs and reindeer. I remember some years back when I was organist in an Anglican cathedral accompanying the congregational singing of Christmas carols. I was perspiring in my robes in the stifling heat while the congregation sang the beautiful carol *In the Bleak Midwinter*.

A shopping mall decked with Christmas decorations.

Another aspect of the European, particularly British, Christmas that does not fit into the New Zealand scene is the traditional Christmas dinner. Roast turkey with lots of hot vegetables and heavy Christmas plum pudding is fine in winter, but in the New Zealand climate in December, light meals and salads are more appropriate. Over the last couple of decades, many Kiwis have seen the logic of this, and the traditional multi-course Christmas dinner has been replaced in many households by lighter and healthier menus. Does that mean that the heavy British fare has disappeared from the Christmas menu? Not at all. The increasingly popular and fun solution is to have a midwinter Christmas dinner as well—but in June or July.

Christmas is also the season for many social occasions. Most firms and organisations usually organise an office party, and I regularly host my immediate staff for lunch in a restaurant as a small thank you for their work during the year. These gestures of thanks are often extended to people who provide services, such as garbage collectors or office cleaners in the form of small presents, such as a bottle of wine or a box of chocolates. There is no obligation to give presents, and also no obligation for you to give a present if you receive one. The same applies to Christmas cards. By all means send some, but it is no longer mandatory, as it used to be, that you must send a card to every person who sends you one.

Many neighbourhoods use Christmas as the season when they organise street parties, where all the neighbours are invited to one of the homes for drinks or a barbecue. It is a good way to extend the compliments of the season to your neighbours, to catch up on street gossip and maintain friendly relations.

Anzac Day

Anzac Day falls on 25 April. ANZAC stands for Australia and New Zealand Army Corps. It is observed in every community of any size and is, perhaps, the most emotional public observance in New Zealand. It commemorates the landing of Australian and New Zealand troops at Gallipoli, Turkey on 30 April 1915 during the First World War, as well as all New Zealanders killed in war. It is also a day to honour service personnel who have returned from active service. The celebrations begin with a dawn service at the local war memorial. This is followed by a parade later in the morning in which the veterans, together with representatives of other community groups and the armed services, march to the memorial for a wreath laying ceremony, which is then followed by a speech made by one of the prominent citizens of the locality. The veterans then adjourn to the local Returned Services Club or a hotel for refreshments and reminiscing. Unlike Waitangi Day, which has often been marred by dissention and protest, Anzac Day has served much more to emphasize the unity of the multiracial New Zealand community. Anti-Vietnam war protesters or women's groups protesting against the suffering imposed by war on defenceless women and children have not been able to impair or destroy the solemnity of this day of remembrance. In recent years, there has been a marked increase in attendance at the ceremonies, particularly by young New Zealanders. It reflects just how important Anzac Day is in the New Zealand psyche. In fact, in 2001, there were debates on whether to abolish the law that prohibits shops from trading on Christmas Day, Good Friday and Easter Sunday, but nobody proposed lifting the prohibition against trading on the morning of Anzac Day.

Other Celebrations

The Queen's Birthday is celebrated simply by having the first Monday in June as a holiday and the announcement of the award of honours to New Zealanders who have given the community particularly distinguished service. There are two other days on which nationwide celebrations take place. The first is Waitangi Day, New Zealand's national day, which commemorates the signing of the Treaty of Waitangi in 1840. For many years, it was celebrated at Waitangi with a major ceremony attended by the governor-general, the prime minister and representatives of the diplomatic corps. After demonstrations by radical Maori minority groups, the focus of the celebrations has shifted to Wellington, although there is still a ceremony at Waitangi. Unlike national day celebrations in many other countries, there are no widespread ceremonies. New Zealanders, on the whole, avoid emotional public rituals unless, of course, as I have already mentioned, they involve one of our national sports teams. A rugby match against arch-foe Australia is usually a pretty emotional affair. In 1995, when New Zealand sailed for the America's Cup, the world's premier yacht racing trophy, the skipper of the New Zealand boat made the comment that during the races, he wore his pair of lucky red socks. Thousands of Kiwis, including me, went out and bought red socks to wear while the regatta was in progress. There is no doubt in my mind that it was these red socks that helped New Zealand win the cup. The triumphant team was also accorded the rare honour of a ticker tape parade through the major New Zealand cities.

Apart from Anzac Day and some Maori family celebrations, you will not see New Zealanders showing much public emotion, as mentioned. The fiery political rhetoric that inflames public meetings, the exuberance of religious festivals, or the extravagance of family celebrations that drive the hosts into debt for many years to come, belong to other cultures. Kiwis are much more down-to-earth and tend to view such spectacles with tolerant but slightly bemused puzzlement. They are good people, the New Zealanders; they will welcome you to their celebrations and occasions with warmth and sincerity. But you will find them restrained if you come from a culture that is rather more flamboyant. Don't let them fool you. Their emotions are just as real and just as genuine and deep as those of your culture.

Fairs and Festivals

In addition to occasional family festivals, religious holidays and national celebrations commemorating significant events in the history of New Zealand, many festivals have been instituted to celebrate particular aspects of New Zealand life. The oldest is probably the Canterbury Agricultural and Pastoral Show, where farmers have been meeting since 1862 to exhibit their cattle and produce and to award prizes for the largest pumpkin or the best pickled onions or the top Friesian heifer. Smaller agricultural and pastoral shows are held throughout the country. Judging these competitions is no laughing matter, and solemn judges in white coats would earnestly consider, for example, the artistic arrangement of Mrs. Jones' bottled peaches. Some of the smaller pastoral shows give a wonderful insight into rural New Zealand. The larger ones, which are listed in the *Calendar of*

Festivals and Holidays at the end of this book, have exhibits that range from the simple produce and animal breeding competitions to the very latest in agricultural machinery and research.

Another typically New Zealand event are the sheepdog trials that take place every year at regional and national levels. Sheepdogs are highly trained animals and work together with the farmer as a team in herding sheep. The competitors are given a number of standardised tasks, such as herding a group of six sheep over a bridge set up in a field in such a way that they can, if they want to, walk beside it, dividing a group of six sheep into two groups of three (this sounds much easier than it actually is!) and then herding the two separate groups into two separate pens. The competition demands great skill from the human and canine participants and is great fun for the spectators, mainly because no matter what the competitor and his dogs want to achieve, the sheep often have other ideas.

While we are talking about agricultural festivals, most country schools hold a 'calf day'. Children from the surrounding farms, who often help with feeding the calves before they are weaned or sold, pick a good specimen and then train it to walk alongside them on a leash. They look after the calf, groom it and generally lavish all their care and attention on it. When the big day arrives, the father hitches the trailer up to the family car, and the calf is transported to the school where there are judges to comment on the grooming, the appearance and the behaviour of the animals (they have to walk down a marked lane on the grass with their young masters). Various coloured ribbons are awarded to the winning animals. Both my younger brothers participated in these calf days, and I remember red and blue ribbons hanging on their bedroom walls long after they had left school.

The calves were turned into prime veal after their brief career in the limelight, or else they ended up a few years later as prime beef. In that form, they may well have been the centrepiece of one of the many wine and food festivals that have become popular in New Zealand. A few years ago, the manager of one of the large hotels in Rotorua, who had worked for the same hotel chain all over the world, told me that in New Zealand, he got the best and freshest ingredients for his kitchens. The trouble he had was that he could not get the staff to do justice to them. This has now changed and both locals and tourists flock to the wine and food festivals all over the country. Perhaps the most attractive festivals are not the ones in the big cities, but those held in the country, in the wine growing regions themselves. For example, in February, Blenheim hosts the Marlborough Food and Wine Festival, and Masterton holds the Wairarapa Wine and Food Festival. The major ones are listed in the *Calendar of Festivals and Holidays* at the back of this book.

Many cultures celebrate public occasions with huge and colourful parades. New Zealanders have some major ones in the large cities at Christmas, when Father Christmas 'comes to town', and at times of great sporting success, such as the America's Cup, the sporting heroes are paraded up the main streets of the cities. In many cities, smaller parades are held in advance of rugby matches, when the local mascot is paraded up the main street to gather public support for the game and, of course, for the local side.

Finally, three aquatic festivals and one that is land-based deserve to be mentioned. The first is the Auckland Anniversary Regatta. This is a sailing regatta that has its origins as far back as 1840, when some boats raced on the harbour to celebrate the raising of the British flag in Auckland. It has been held every year since then and was only cancelled once, in 1900, because of the war that was then raging in South Africa. With thousands of boats on the harbour, the regatta is the largest one-day regatta in the world. There are races that range from world-class racing yachts right down to tiny radio-controlled model boats. It certainly is a spectacular event.

The second regatta is on the Waikato River, at Ngaruawahia, the seat of the Maori queen, north of Hamilton. It is a Maori event, but everybody is welcome. There are not only Maori canoe races, but horse swimming, rowing and motor boat racing, as well as Maori dance and cultural competitions. This regatta, just like the one in Auckland, is a spectacle that should not be missed if you want to see a typical New Zealand celebration.

The third regatta is also held on the Waikato River and is just becoming established as an event. It is called the Great Race and is held in September. It is an offshoot of the great race held annually between the rowing teams of Oxford and Cambridge universities in England. One of these teams is invited to New Zealand and then races against a team put up by the University of Waikato in Hamilton.

The fourth festival is land-based and is held every year in Auckland. The Pasifika Polynesian Festival is said to be the largest such festival in the world. The festival is attended by about 140,000 people who come to watch Polynesian singing and dancing, to hear the latest music produced, to enjoy Pacific ethnic food, to watch traditional craft demonstrations; in short, to have a great time. I have attended it and was struck by the fact that here was a microcosm of all the colour, noise and exuberance of the Polynesian people on the outskirts of the largest Polynesian city in the world. Join them if you can. It is well worth it.

Chapter Three

HAERE MAI

ARRIVAL

Captain Cook's surgeon's boy, Nicholas Young, first spotted the coast of New Zealand from the crow's nest of Cook's ship, the *Endeavour*. The promontory near Gisborne on the eastern coast of the North Island that he is supposed to have seen was accordingly named 'Young Nick's Head', a name that it bears to this day. It was the second time that the promontory had been named by a famous captain. The Maori name, *Te Kuri a Paoa*, was bestowed on it by Paoa, the captain of the *Horouta* voyaging canoe. Unlike Cook, he named it after his dog!

I first saw New Zealand from the deck of the ship that brought me to this country with my family. It was October, and Wellington harbour was obscured by a rain squall that suddenly lifted like the curtain on a stage, revealing the city bathed in early morning sunshine. I cannot boast that any coastal feature is named after me —the names had all been allocated by the time I arrived, first by Maori and then by the European colonisers. There have been some moves in recent times to restore some of the original place names that have been changed by Europeans, so you will find that, for example, Mount Egmont now also bears the original Maori name Mount Taranaki.

Your first glimpse of the country is likely to be from the window of an aircraft that has flown for at least two hours over the sea. If you are like me, and if this is your first visit to New Zealand, you will be slightly apprehensive about what you will encounter once you cross the airbridge into the airport terminal and what lies beyond.

You will already have had a slight taste of what you will find because you will have been handed a form to fill in for immigration, customs and agriculture. In my view, it is a bit more user-friendly than the form you have to fill in as you approach the United States where you are asked to tick a box after the statement: 'I am, or have been, engaged in espionage activity' –yes/no. I cannot help it, but every time I fill out the form, I am tempted to tick 'yes', and see what happens.

I am assuming that your visa is in order, and that you are not carrying lethal weapons or any other doomsday gear. You will see on the form however, that there are many questions relating to items of food and other natural products, such as wood, feathers, seeds and soil, etc. As New Zealand consists of a number of islands and because, as we have seen, more than two-thirds of our exports are primary produce, our biosecurity laws are extremely strict and any breach is punished severely. I know that it is comforting to have food from home, but I would suggest that you check very carefully whether anything you would like to bring is permitted. Even a seasoned traveller like me can at times be surprised. Some years ago I visited Hungary and bought one of those wonderful, large, tasty Hungarian salami which I then dragged along with me all over Europe. Not one of the many countries I visited was concerned, until I arrived at the Auckland airport. Like any responsible citizen I had, of course, declared it, and when I got to the checkpoint and the officer saw it, he sadly but firmly informed me that I was not allowed to bring it into the country and he deeply regretted having to take it off me.

I see we have already landed and have gone through the checks. (I, minus my salami, you, without having had anything confiscated because you carefully observed my advice). If you have arranged for someone to meet you, then you can now relax and let your friend take you to the place where you intend staying. If not, you may need some initial accommodation, and you will obviously need to get there.

Hotels and Motels

New Zealand is currently enjoying a tourist boom and this means that there is plenty of accommodation ranging from backpackers to five-star hotels (which however, are only found in major cities and tourist resorts). By world standards, prices are quite reasonable. Where you spend your first night in New Zealand depends a bit on your preferences. If you want to stay in the city centre of one of the major cities, you would probably choose a hotel. Most New Zealanders would probably stay in a motel, in a self-contained unit complete with a little kitchen in which you can prepare your own meals. These are generally cheaper than hotels, but since most of them are designed for people who have their own cars (or a rental car), they are sometimes not within easy walking distance of the central business district of the major cities. Some of the larger, and more expensive ones, will have restaurants attached to them. The more modest ones will usually serve breakfast only, and you will have to cook your own meals or find a restaurant. All international airports have information counters where you can find accommodation to suit you if you have not booked ahead.

A motel is a cheaper alternative to a hotel.

Leaving the Airport and Onwards

There are usually buses or shuttles from the airport to town, or else you can take a taxi. Taxis in New Zealand are metered, and I have found the drivers to be generally helpful and honest. Taxi stands are located at airports and dotted throughout most larger cities. You can also hail a taxi from the kerbside by waving out to it. It is usually helpful (and also safer) if you choose a place to hail a taxi that does not involve holding up other traffic.

You can, of course, also rent a car at the airport if you are happy to brave the traffic. We drive on the left side of the road in New Zealand, and traffic is quite well controlled, compared with many cities in more populous countries. In the end, it is a matter of personal preference, and when I land in a city for the first time, I generally prefer to let someone who is familiar with the traffic and the geography, like a bus or taxi driver, take me to my destination.

Well, it looks as if we have arrived at our lodgings for the night. Perhaps there is time to take a bit of a walk (or drive, if you are adventurous) before going to bed, and you will most likely find the neighbourhood clean, orderly and uncrowded. Some years ago we entertained a couple who had lived most of their lives in England. As we walked around the streets in our suburb, Bill, the husband, kept on walking out into the empty street, exclaiming "Where are all the people, where are all the people?" He was lucky not to be run over by a car, because Kiwi drivers are accustomed to having the road to themselves and therefore are often not as attentive as drivers in more populous countries. By all means, go for an exploratory walk, but take care all the same, because we need to be in one piece tomorrow for settling into this new, exciting country.

SETTLING IN

If you are going to settle in the city in which you arrived, or if you flew directly after arriving at the international airport to the provincial city where you are going to live, you are ready to start settling in as soon as you have got over the jetlag. If you have to travel to the place of your work or study, have a look at the next chapter under 'Getting Around' for some tips about travelling within New Zealand. Let's assume that you are now in the town where you are going to settle and need to find long-term accommodation.

New Zealand Homes

Kiwis love to live in their own homes; indeed New Zealand has one of the highest home ownership rates in the world. Almost 70% of New Zealanders own their own house or apartment. Most homes are single-family bungalows built of wood or brick and surrounded by a garden. In the cities, you can purchase or rent apartments in apartment blocks. Because of the moderate climate, New Zealand houses do not normally have central heating or air conditioning, although many shops and office buildings do. If you are renting, the landlord is not obliged to provide heating. You may have to buy a heater yourself. You will certainly need one. Winter evenings can be quite chilly, and there will be frosts on some winter nights south of Auckland. We do not heat our house during the daytime, but we are glad to have our woodburner heater in the evenings, and some electric heaters to take the chill of the mornings. Again, because of the moderate climate, New Zealand houses are fairly lightly-built and the majority are single-storied. There is no huge attic; in fact, there is no real attic at all. Combined with the most common form of roofing—galvanized iron sheets—this means that when it rains, the noise is quite audible, and during heavy rain, you will have to turn up the volume on your TV if you want to hear what is going on.

It does not matter whether you are a wealthy immigrant with hundreds of thousands of dollars to spend on a palatial home or a rather poor student looking for budget accommodation, your first source of information is most probably the newspaper. The best days to look for classified advertisements either under 'Houses, Land for Sale' or under 'To let' are on a Wednesday and Saturday. In the paper,

A medium-priced house.

and in the Yellow Pages of the local telephone directory, you will also find listings for real estate agents (which are probably your best bet if you are thinking of buying a house). Many of them also have rental properties, called 'flats', available and will charge you a week's rent plus GST (the Goods and Services Tax of 12.5%) for finding you a rental property.

Renting

If you choose to rent, you will find that most rental properties are unfurnished. These properties may be houses, complete with the garden around them. If they are flats, they can be older houses that have been divided into a number of apartments, or else they are purpose-built structures, typically containing from two to 20 units of one-or two-bedroom apartments. You will need to sign a tenancy agreement with the landlord. The landlord can ask you to pay a 'bond', a sum of money that can be no more than four weeks' rent (it is usual to ask for two or three weeks' rent). This sum will be refunded to you when you end the tenancy unless you are either behind with the rent or have caused some damage to the flat. Rent is generally paid fortnightly in advance. Your responsibility is to keep the flat clean and tidy. Your landlord is responsible for maintaining the property, so if anything needs to be repaired, you should let them or their agent know immediately. Your landlord will also pay any taxes and insurance in respect of the property. You will have to pay for electricity, gas, telephone and water.

When you arrive in your rented house or flat, you may find a telephone that is not connected because the previous tenants had it disconnected when they left. You will need to ring New Zealand Telecom from another telephone to have your phone connected again. The number is given in the *Resource Guide* at the end of this book. Provided there is a phone and line in your apartment, and provided satisfactory credit arrangements are in place, New Zealand Telecom will usually connect you within 24 hours. You will have to pay a monthly fee for the telephone, but that fee includes all your local calls, so you will be billed only for long distance calls and any extra services to which you may choose to subscribe.

You will find that in virtually all cases, the water is connected, but you may have to make arrangements to be hooked up to electricity and gas. Your best source of information is probably your landlord or landlady who will know which of the local suppliers have been used before. If they are not available, ask the real estate agent that has found you the property. Failing that, check in the Yellow Pages of you telephone book under 'Electricity Supply Retail', and in the White Pages under 'Natural Gas Corporation'. The latter will however only inform you whether there is gas piped to your area. The best source for finding the local gas provider would be the shop that sells you the appliance that you may want to connect to it.

If you want to leave, you will have to give three weeks' written notice to the landlord, while your landlord is obliged by law to give you three months (90 days) written notice if they want you to vacate the premises. They need only give you 6 weeks (42 days) notice if they wish to use the premises for their family or employees or if they have sold the property and have agreed to hand it over vacant. They must also inform you why they did not give you 90 days notice. You do have rights under New Zealand law as a tenant, and these can be enforced if necessary. When you leave, you will have to make sure all the services are disconnected and pay any outstanding bills.

Provided you are a good tenant and your landlord (like the majority of them) is reasonable, you should have no problems with rented accommodation. In case you do, however, some useful addresses, including that of the Ministry of Housing (Tenancy Services), are given in the *Resource Guide* at the end of this book.

Buying a House

If you are in a position to buy a house, my advice would be to take some time over it, simply to make sure that you have selected the

house and the area of the town that you really want to live in. If you have children or are elderly, you will need to think about schools, access to medical care and shopping when you decide where to look for a house. New Zealand state schools have zones, and if you live in a particular neighbourhood, your children normally cannot go to a school in another zone. It may be a good idea if you start by renting a house. This will remove the pressure to buy quickly (and possibly avoid a costly mistake) and will also give you and your family an idea of what you like and what you don't like in a New Zealand house.

There are a wide variety of houses in New Zealand. They range from modest two-bedroom cottages to architect-designed palaces. Foreign visitors to New Zealand have told me that they find New Zealand houses rather unimaginative and drab and, within reason, they have a point. Because New Zealanders like to live in their own homes, they had to find a way to acquire them even with the modest amounts of money they earn. This has led to the development of simple houses, all of them with identical floor plans that could be built cheaply and efficiently. In the second half of the 20th century, many thousands of such houses were built. In fact, we rented one until we

Cheap mass-produced housing.

could afford to build our own home. Incidentally, the Number-8-wire mentality had influenced me by that stage. Bored with the stock plans I had perused when contemplating building a home, I finally designed my own (architectural and drafting training—NIL!), took it to a builder who made the necessary adjustments to ensure that it complied with the building code, and then built it. We have lived in it happily for more than 30 years now!

As in other countries, house architecture in New Zealand is subject to fashion. The stock basic houses, the so-called Mediterranean- or Spanish-style houses which were all the rage some decades ago, are characterised by rounded doorways and pergolas. At the moment, the preferred style for upmarket housing is for rounded roofs and grand entrance ways with two-storey-high columns holding up a canopy over the main door. Another recent development is the advent of what is called 'infill' housing. The large plots of land (called 'sections') are subdivided for a second house to be built. Blocks of townhouses and apartments can be built on such land in larger cities. This reflects the trend towards a higher housing density.

But there are still plenty of modest, mass-produced, simple single-family houses on plenty of land for the children to romp around and the parents to grow their own vegetables. An old-style, wooden colonial mansion with wide verandas, surrounded by mature trees and huge Rhododendron bushes, may charm you as well. Just don't forget that wooden houses will require regular painting, and the bigger the house, the bigger, more expensive and time-consuming the job. To you, this may suggest higher costs for painters and paint, and this is certainly true. For most Kiwis however, it suggests many more hours standing on ladders and trestles since many New Zealanders paint their own homes. I still remember one of my university professors giving classes with specks of white paint in his hair because he was painting his house.

A garage sale is usually a good place to find bargain items.

While buying and selling a house in New Zealand is a comparatively simple process, it is advisable to use a real estate agent and a lawyer to make sure that you receive appropriate advice and that your interests are protected. They can also advise you on sources of finance and explain the various stages involved in the process.

Furnishing a Home

Whether you rent or buy, you will need some furniture for your new home, and again, depending on your circumstances, you have choices. If you can afford to buy new furniture, there are numerous furniture stores that sell quality goods. If you are here only temporarily or if your budget does not allow you to get new articles, there are plenty of second-hand shops that will allow you to furnish your flat or house relatively cheaply. There are however, some other alternatives for getting cheap second-hand goods. One of them is the garage sale which has become a feature of New Zealand weekends. Garage sales are organised by individuals (or sometimes a group of neighbours), and are usually advertised in Friday's newspaper. When you go to the private address, you will find that the garage contains all sorts of second-hand goods and bric-a-brac that the owner wants to get rid of. You can bargain, if you want to, and make an offer. The important thing about garage sales is that you must go early because most of the good pieces will get sold to early birds (those that get there first), and if you get there around lunchtime, you will only find the things that nobody else wants.

Every Thursday, a publication called *Loot* appears in bookstores, supermarkets and petrol stations. It contains advertisements for second-hand goods. The January sales are also a good time to buy things like new linen and kitchen utensils at a reasonable price. Most towns and cities also have Opportunity Shops. These are usually run by volunteers to raise money for charity. They can also be a good source of used goods and clothes.

Major consumer items, such as washing machines, television sets and refrigerators, come in a startling array of models and prices. *The New Zealand Consumer* magazine regularly publishes the results of tests they conduct on household appliances and other consumer goods. While you will not get the detailed results of the tests on the magazine's website (which is listed in the *Resource Guide*), you will be able to access them if you subscribe to the magazine, either the electronic version or the more traditional paper copy. If you do not wish to subscribe to the magazine, it will always be available, free-of-charge, in your local public library.

Buying a Car

Probably the most expensive acquisition after a house, if you buy one, will be your car. You will almost certainly need one because public transport in New Zealand, as we shall see in a later chapter, is not very good, and you will be rather hampered if you have to rely on trains and buses to get around. You may want to buy a new car, and most brands are available in New Zealand, with Japanese cars predominating. If you buy the car second-hand, you will find that most of the cars on offer will be imported second-hand Japanese cars. You may choose to buy a car from a private seller. The best days to look for advertisements are on Wednesday and Saturday. Unless you are a motor mechanic, I would strongly suggest that you have it checked (for a fee) by a garage or the Automobile Association, whose website is listed in the *Resource Guide*. It would also be advisable to check that there is no money outstanding on the car, since some unscrupulous sellers will try and sell the car before they have paid it off.

The legal requirements for selling a car are given in a fact sheet on the website of the New Zealand Land Transport Safety Authority that you will find in the *Resource Guide*. Other useful advice on buying a car is on the website of the Ministry of Consumer Affairs that is also listed in the *Resource Guide*. Incidentally, if you buy a second-hand car from a motor vehicle dealer, it is a good idea to use a dealer that has the acronym LMVD (Licensed Motor Vehicle Dealer) behind their firm's name. The dealer will also take care of the legal formalities. While you should still be careful, buying from a dealer is generally considered to be a bit safer than buying privately.

Another possibility for finding the car you want is at a New Zealand car fair. The organisers hire a large space; for example, the parking lot of a race course, and people who want to sell their car bring it there at the time of the fair, which is usually on Saturday morning. They pay a fee for being able to display their car. Buyers can then stroll up and down the rows of cars for sale, inspect and negotiate and end up with a good bargain. Two of the points made earlier apply here. Firstly, I would strongly advise a thorough mechanical inspection, and secondly, the early bird gets the worm—the best deals are likely to be struck by early arrivals.

Finally, there are also car auctions in the larger cities. After having a look at the catalogue and some of the cars, you can arrange for a mechanical inspection (preferably on the day before the auction), and take the car for a drive. It is a good idea to determine beforehand how much you will bid for the vehicle you have chosen, and then stick to your bid. If you do not feel comfortable bidding yourself, you can get one of the staff of the auctioneer to bid for you. Any goods you buy at an auction must be paid for in full by cash, bank cheque or credit card on the day of the auction or, in the case of an evening auction, by noon on the following day. Payment terms vary depending on the auction house.

A Note on Toilet Etiquette

Let's assume that you have now settled into your home. You may need just a few words of advice about New Zealand toilets and bathrooms. New Zealand uses Western toilets, which means that men either sit on the toilet seat or lift up the hinged seat and stand in front of the toilet bowl to urinate. Women always sit.

Most people use toilet paper rather than water to clean themselves, and toilets are flushed after each use. The toilet paper is flushed down the toilet, but women's sanitary products are disposed of in a special rubbish bin that is usually found in the toilet.

Do not splash the toilet with water after you have used it, and never stand on the toilet seat. To shower, you stand under the continuously flowing water. A friend of mine from a country where showers were not common at first used to take a bucket into the shower with him. He would then fill the bucket with warm water from the shower, turn off the water and then tip the water over himself. It did not take him long to learn that there was an easier way!

Homestays

One option for living in New Zealand, particularly if you come as a student, is to arrange for a homestay. Your school or university will be able to advise you about homestay accommodation, and they will have screened homestay hosts. What it means is that you live in a private home as a lodger. This has its many advantages, as you will have more opportunities to practise English and also see how a typical New Zealand family lives. There are however, a few pitfalls that you should avoid.

A homestay coordinator that I talked with told me that one of the biggest issues to be clarified right from the start is food. Unlike when you live in your own accommodation and can cook for yourself, the homestay family will provide the food, and it will be New Zealand fare. There will be plenty of it and it will be of good quality, but you will have to be aware that New Zealanders fill up on bread, potatoes and pasta, while you may be used to rice. Also, your host family would like you to be 'one of the family', so if you are thirsty, don't wait for them to offer you a glass of water; it is perfectly acceptable for you to get one yourself.

Many New Zealand families have pets, mainly dogs or cats. If in your culture pets are not liked or are culturally offensive, you will have to request a homestay family that does not have any pets. The important thing is that you make these arrangements beforehand. The homestay coordinators can usually accommodate you if they know your requirements. If they don't, and you only make your needs known once you have arrived and have been allocated a host family, making changes is more difficult.

Finally, it pays not to arrive with unrealistic expectations. A homestay family is not a five-star hotel, and as I have already mentioned, New Zealand families do not have servants. So it is very much appreciated if you help sometimes with the chores, such as drying dishes after a meal. This is not only appreciated as a gesture of 'being one of the family', it is also another opportunity for you to practise your English with your hosts.

A second unrealistic expectation is that the home will be within a few minutes' walk of the inner city. Most homestay hosts live in the suburbs, sometimes quite a long way from the bright lights of the central business district. Bus services are not very frequent, so you may have to do some careful planning if you are going out.

I hope that all these points have not put you off considering homestay. New Zealanders are warm and friendly people. They will welcome you into their homes, and many overseas students have made lifelong friends by choosing this way of lodging.

MAKING FRIENDS

I have already mentioned that because of the relative geographic isolation of New Zealand, most young Kiwis, after they have completed their education, go on what is known here as OE (overseas experience), the extended overseas trip that may take a few months or a few years. Most of them then return to New Zealand to settle down. It is quite possible that some of the Kiwis you encounter will have been to the country from which you came. They will certainly know what culture shock feels like.

New Zealanders are, on the whole, outgoing gregarious people, and it is not difficult to strike up a conversation with most of them. The person sitting next to you in the bus, in the doctor's waiting room, or in the supermarket checkout queue will often quite happily strike up a conversation with you even though you may be complete strangers.

It is true, however, that at times Kiwis, like the bird after which they are named, can be a bit shy, particularly when they meet people from different cultures who also can look different from the Caucasian or Polynesian mix that they normally find in New Zealand. This has nothing to do with racial prejudice; it is simply due to an insecurity about how to 'deal' with this foreign-looking person who perhaps does not speak English well and may have difficulty understanding the New Zealand accent. I have observed my students and found that this initial reticence on the part of the Kiwis sometimes leads to the foreign students, particularly if they are from Asian countries, withdrawing into their group. This is a pity because both the Kiwis and the foreign students can learn so much from each other, and I have seen some very good friendships develop once the initial reserve has been overcome.

The important lesson in this is that both sides will have to take some steps to become acquainted and this involves sometimes taking some small risks. It certainly involves making use of occasions where social contact is necessary, such as morning and afternoon tea breaks at work, work functions, or student social gatherings if you are a student. Sometimes it may be necessary for you to take the initiative (and thus risking a rebuff) and invite some Kiwis to your home. I know it is not easy, but if you persist it will be well worth it.

One way of meeting people who live around you is to be a 'good neighbour'. Most New Zealanders like to meet their neighbours and to establish a friendly and supportive relationship with them. That does not mean that you have to make friends with someone you would not normally mix with. It can start with a simple introduction. When we went to greet our newly arrived Chinese neighbours recently, they told us that they were not quite sure whether it was acceptable for them to come to us and introduce themselves. It is quite all right for you to take the initiative. Choose a time that is not too early or too late and not at a mealtime to personally visit your neighbour and say hello. Once you are introduced, a warm and friendly hello when you see each other is all that is needed. You can ask about the routines of the neighbourhood, such as garbage collection (in New Zealand, garbage is called 'rubbish'), and newspaper, mail and milk delivery times.

You can become a considerate neighbour by not making a loud noise too early (say, before 8:00 a.m.), or too late (after 11:00 p.m.) Lawnmowers and chain saws can be a major irritant if used inconsiderately. At the same time, your neighbours will appreciate it if you keep your lawn mowed and your garden tidy. For those of you who come from a large city where you have never had a garden, this may be a bit difficult. How do you cope with a hedge that threatens to take over your whole house? When do you plant vegetables and when do you prune your citrus trees? You can ask at your local garden centre; the people working there often are enthusiasts and will be very happy to advise you. Your neighbours also will, in most cases, be pleased if you ask them for advice. Just ask them—you will be surprised how knowledgeable they are or, at least, appear to be!

You are entitled to cut back any branches of trees or shrubs that cross the fence into you property, but it is a good idea to talk to you neighbour first. You will also have to clear away anything you have cut off, unless your neighbour offers to do it for you. Do not light any rubbish fires in your backyard. This can be a major irritant and could spoil good neighbourly relations. If you are planning a big social event, there will inevitably be some noise. Let your neighbours know in advance—you may even invite some of them if you wish. Most neighbours are happy to tolerate some extra noise on the odd occasion if they have been warned in advance.

A good neighbourly thing is to share surplus produce from your garden. Don't be afraid to ask for help in identifying what is a plant and what is a weed. Our Chinese neighbours were very grateful when we pointed out some plants to them that were weeds, and they got rid of them promptly, which we appreciated.

Let your neighbours know if you are going away. Many of them will be happy to keep an eye on your house and even water plants or mind any pet animals. You can return the favour when they are away.

Clubs and Associations

One way of making Kiwi friends is to join a club if you have a particular hobby or interest. Sports clubs are particularly popular, but there are clubs for every conceivable pastime. Even cage bird keeping, cake decorating, and salt and pepper shaker collecting are catered for in a directory of clubs that I have in front of me. If you live in Hamilton, you could also join 'Alf's Imperial Fifth Waikato Dragoons'. It lists as its aim to 'promote modern Victorianism, especially as it relates to pacifist warfare'. (If you can't make sense of this, don't worry, neither can I!) The best way to find out what clubs there are in your area is to ask the local Citizens Advice Bureau or go to the website of the local city council. Don't be misled by the name Citizens Advice Bureau. It is not only for New Zealand 'citizens' but for anybody living in the area, and it can help you not only with clubs, but also, on a free and confidential basis, with advice on education, legal issues, housing and tenancy problems, health and welfare; in short, with any problem where you need free authoritative advice. The nationwide telephone number where you can find the office nearest to you is listed in the back of this book in the *Resource Guide*.

In many of the major cities, you will also find that churches and other organisations have started English conversation groups for new settlers, some of them free of charge. By joining one of these, you will not only improve your English, but you will also meet people who are

The Citizens Advice Bureau is a good place to get information and advice.

in a similar situation to you. Again, the Citizens Advice Bureau can give you the relevant information or you can go to the website of organizations such as the ESOL Home Tutor Service that is given in the *Resource Guide* at the end of this book. The Home Tutor Service not only organises English tuition, it also runs English conversation groups, groups for special purposes, social gatherings and outings.

A way to make friends and learn a new skill as well is by joining one of the many voluntary organisations that will be operating in your neighbourhood. If you have a car, you may want to become a driver for the 'Meals on Wheels' programme, an organisation that distributes meals to elderly or immobile people. Or you may apply to be selected and trained for a counselling agency that uses volunteer counsellors. Alternatively, you may want to join agencies such as Literacy Aotearoa that provides tuition for adults who have literacy problems. There are numerous voluntary organizations, and your local Citizens Advice Bureau will be able to advise you about what is available in your area.

Sometimes it also helps to get in touch with people from the country you have come from. They can be a source of comfort and help, particularly in the early days. If you have no connections through private contacts, the Citizens Advice Bureau can help with a list of various international groups. My home city, Hamilton, for example, has a list of 72 international groups or clubs. Again, it takes a little courage to pick up the phone and ring a total stranger, even if they come from the same country that you do. But go ahead and take the risk. It will be well worth it!

If all else fails, if there is nobody from you country in the town that you live, if there is no Sword Swallower Society nearby, I would encourage you to take the initiative yourself. I have recently heard the story of an immigrant from Asia who was a bit lonely and who also was qualified in one of the many martial arts practised in her country. So she put an advertisement in the local paper offering instruction for women in self-defence. She now has a group of students of varying ages and from all walks of life that is turning into a group of friends.

A recent and very welcome development has been the advent of special programmes, offered by private providers, to help new settlers in New Zealand to settle in and find their place. If you feel that you need some help, check out the Kiwi Ora Programme. The website is listed in the *Resource Guide* at the end of this book under *Advice*.

It can be easy to make friends with New Zealanders once you have broken down that initial shyness and resulting reserve. Go out there and meet them! Take a few risks! You will be amply rewarded.

Pets

You may want to acquire a pet for company, since not all friends need to be of the human species. I would not advise you to bring your pet with you. To bring along your dog or cat requires a permit, and then you will have to board them for a minimum period of 120 days in a registered quarantine facility, which is not cheap.

Dogs, cats, caged birds and goldfish are the most common pets in New Zealand, although dogs, as we have seen, are also used as working animals on farms. Most major cities have pet shops where you can buy pets, but often kittens are advertised in the newspaper for free, or the local Cats Protection League will place abandoned cats in good homes. We got ours that way.

Of course you will want to look after your pet. But what do you do if you are going to be away for a few days? Here is where the good neighbour comes in again. We have lived next door to the same family for many years and regularly look after each other's cats when either of us is away. You may want to do the same. As an alternative, there are pet minding businesses—kennels and catteries—that will board your pet for a fee.

THE SOCIAL ROUND

I have attended many social occasions in New Zealand, and they have ranged from a gathering with a few friends around a television set for

A barbecue is a pleasant way to enjoy an evening outdoors with friends.

a few beers and a football game, to a formal reception for an overseas head of state hosted by the prime minister. I hasten to add that most occasions to which I am invited are at the lower end of the spectrum!

Kiwis have, as we have observed several times already, an informal society, and that also applies to their social occasions. One of the favourite forms of entertaining in summer is the barbecue, a meal cooked outdoors on a charcoal or (increasingly) gas grill, where steaks, sausages, kebabs, seafood and other delicacies are prepared while the guests stand or sit around sipping beer or wine. The meat is usually served with salads. It is a delightful way to entertain and be entertained.

If you are invited to a barbecue, you would dress informally; men in open neck shirts and slacks or jeans, ladies in slacks and a simple top. I tend to prefer to wear longs, although short trousers would be

85

acceptable for men. This is simply because towards the evening, sandflies (tiny, stinging insects) tend to become active, and I like to avoid having to slap my legs all the time. Hosts will often provide insect repellent for their guests, but I suggest you take some yourself as a precaution.

It also pays to make sure what to bring. Some barbecues are communal efforts, where the host provides the grill and the guests contribute the meat, salads, etc. For others, the host provides everything down to the paper serviettes. When you are invited, the question "Is there anything you would like me to bring?" will normally get you the information you need. What they will not tell you to bring is something to drink. It is however, polite to bring along a bottle of wine or some beer and hand it to the host on arrival. If you are a teetotaller, some fruit juice is fine. Always ask what time you are expected to arrive. You can take your cue from the other guests about when it is appropriate to leave.

For barbecues and other informal social occasions, it is usually fine to arrive 10 to 15 minutes late. If you arrive exactly at the time for which you were invited, you are likely to be the first arrival and will therefore have to carry the conversational burden until the next guests arrive. My Kiwi wife and I show our different cultural backgrounds in this. Having been brought up in Switzerland, I tend to want to be on time, while she observes the normal New Zealand delay. So I champ at the bit while she hangs back when we go to a social function. Fortunately, we have been married long enough to have come to terms with each other's idiosyncrasies, so that we don't arrive at the party gouging each other's eyes out and screaming abuse at each other. We usually agree to compromise!

You may be invited to a 'pot luck dinner'. This is a dinner where every guest brings a dish which is then shared with the other guests. Again, this is in anformal occasion and you also might want to ask the hosts what to bring to ensure that not everybody brings a dessert. Pot luck dinners are good occasions to bring a dish from your culture.

Greeting a Kiwi

When you arrive, you will be welcomed by the hosts and introduced to the other guests. To greet them, it is customary in New Zealand to shake hands firmly and look into the eyes of the person you are meeting. Among the older generation, men always shake hands, but women are less likely to shake hands with the men they are introduced to but simply smile. I always take my cue from the woman I'm encountering. If she puts out her hand, I shake it, if not, I smile. Over the last few years, New Zealanders have dropped some of their reserve inherited from the British, and if you are good friends and of opposite genders, it is quite acceptable to have a quick hug and a kiss on the cheek, both on arrival and on parting. As always, take your cue from the person you are greeting and tell them if this is culturally inappropriate for you. This will not cause any offence.

New Zealanders like plenty of personal space. So when you talk to them in a social setting, standing on the lawn or in a room, make sure that you leave plenty of space between you and them. I have a colleague who comes from another culture where people stand much closer together. He is also much more volatile and excitable than the normally placid Kiwi. I have often watched him with amusement having a conversation with a New Zealand partner. He will stand far too close, and then get excited and start waving his hands about. The Kiwi will start moving backwards to establish what for him is a comfortable distance, the colleague will advance with flailing arms, the Kiwi will retreat further, until, inevitably, he is manoeuvred into a corner with my colleague looming over him like an excited bird of prey. I have learned to avoid him on social occasions!

Most of the 'rules' that apply to barbecues also apply to other social occasions. Dinner parties are also generally informal and you dress informally for them, perhaps just slightly 'up' from the barbecue. Again, it is customary to bring along either a bottle of wine, some flowers, or a box of chocolates as a gift.

Table Etiquette
Like most Western societies, New Zealanders use forks, spoons and knives to eat, and they will be just as forgiving when you have difficulty handling them as are my Asian hosts when I make an exhibition of myself trying to pick up a sliver of slithery mushroom with my chopsticks. The days when lots of special cutlery was used have long since gone, but if there are several courses to the dinner, you will find several sets of cutlery laid out for you. Just work your way in from the outside. The outermost set will be for the entrée, which is the course before the main course, not, as in the United States, the main course. The next set will be for the main course. Cutlery for the dessert will often be laid across the top of the plate. To avoid making a faux pas, I suggest you do what I do when I am in an unfamiliar setting for a meal: watch the host or hostess and do as they do.

There is a convention with cutlery during a meal that is not observed universally, but is certainly still current in 'refined' households. When you have finished the main course, you may indicate that you would be quite happy to have some more by putting down your knife and fork crossed on your plate. If you would like to indicate that you have had enough, place them parallel along the side of the plate. But whatever you do, never put a used set of cutlery down on the table cloth. Always put them on the plate.

If you are asked whether you would like a 'second helping', i.e. more food, it is perfectly all right to accept if you feel like it or to decline if you have had enough. As I have already mentioned, New Zealanders don't have servants, and the meal will have been cooked by the host or hostess. The greatest compliment you can pay a New Zealand home cook is to ask for the recipe.

A fun way of sharing in each other's culture is to offer to bring or offer to cook one of your special dishes. A Chinese student who spent Christmas Day with us recently brought along some home-made wontons and cooked them in a large pot. We greatly enjoyed them along with the cold turkey and ham and the various summer salads.

Dinners are usually followed by coffee, which is normally the signal that the party is over and it is time to go home. This is not always the case though, and some hosts like to linger over coffee. It is probably best to take the cue from any other guests.

Drop Ins

Neighbours and friends will often call on each other just for a 'quick chat'. They will, in New Zealand speak, 'drop in'. Don't be surprised if they come to the back door of the house rather than to the front door, which often is used for the more 'formal' occasions. There is no social obligation on you to serve them any food. If it is around morning and afternoon tea time, you may invite them for a cup of tea. Say something like, "I was just going to make a cup of tea/coffee, would you like one?" They will probably say something like they "don't want to be any trouble". If you assure them that you were making a drink anyway, they will probably be happy to have one. If they refuse, don't be offended. The informal New Zealand social scene does not have any rules about what constitutes acceptable hospitality.

Etiquette at Maori Functions

If you are invited to a Maori function, say a wedding or a funeral (*tangi*), you will, as I have already mentioned, be welcomed to the *marae* in a group. You will therefore assemble outside with the other guests and wait to be conducted in. During the welcome, the visiting group of which you are a member, will present the *koha*, which is usually money, to help the hosts with the expenses associated with the hosting. While waiting outside, you will see someone going around with an envelope and he (it is usually a man) will take your contribution and later present it, together with the others, to the hosts. If you are unsure about how much to contribute, a discreet inquiry to one of the other guests will solve the problem and save anxiety.

And while we are talking about polite behaviour in a Maori setting, just a couple more hints. When food is served, and it inevitably will be, and if you are a guest of a Maori family, it is customary for a senior member of the group to say grace before the meal. This is generally said in Maori and you should not start to eat before the *karakia* has been said. Also, Maori find it most offensive if you sit on a table where food has been served or may be served later. The best thing to do is simply never to sit on a table in a Maori setting. Finally, never touch a Maori's head with you hands. This is the most sacred part of their body and must not be touched. I remember a couple of years ago going to a performance of the famous Canadian circus *Cirque du Soleil* in Auckland. In the opening number, the band with a few clowns marched through the audience, with the clowns affectionately ruffling the hair of the people. Clearly they meant no harm: it simply was a friendly gesture. For a Maori however, this would be quite inappropriate.

The Ride Home

If you intend to drive home from whatever social occasion you have been to, you will need to be very careful about your consumption of alcohol or else have a member of your group who has been chosen as the sober driver. New Zealand has very strict laws relating to drinking and driving, and heavy penalties including fines, suspension of your driver's licence, confiscation of the vehicle and even imprisonment are imposed on drivers who are over the limit. Police can stop any driver at random and test their blood alcohol level, and checkpoints are set up regularly, any time of the day or night, to check all motorists. So if you are going to drive home from that barbecue or dinner party, do not risk losing your licence, your money or even your life. It simply isn't worth it! Nobody is immune from these checks, by the way.

As I have already mentioned, we drive on the left side of the road in New Zealand, which means that the steering wheel is on the right side of the car. There is a story about a police patrol seeing a driver drive erratically one night and stopping the car for a breath test for alcohol. The person in the car wound down the window, blew into the bag and returned a negative test. No alcohol whatever! The policemen let him drive off, but as they followed him, he was still driving erratically. So they stopped and tested him again. Again negative! They stopped the car a third time, shone their torch into it and found that it was an American car with the steering wheel on the right hand side. They had tested the passenger twice and not the driver who was indeed badly affected by alcohol and, in due course, got his just desserts.

But enough of rules of behaviour. As I said at the beginning of this section, New Zealanders are delightfully informal, and as long as you stick to the few suggestions I have given, there is very little that you can do wrong. If there is something that they do wrong, that is if some of their behaviours or food items are culturally inappropriate for you, just politely tell them that your religion will not permit you, for example, to eat pork, or be on your own in a room with a man, they will not take offence. To successfully participate in the social round of New Zealand, you must do whatever a good communicator does: ask for all the information you need to be comfortable, and give all the information your host needs to be comfortable with you. You will give your hosts the most pleasure if you relax and enjoy yourself.

Inviting Kiwis to Your Home

There will be a time when you would like to be the host and invite some Kiwis to your home. Unless it is a formal occasion, such as a major birthday celebration, invitations are usually not extended formally by letter. Most often, they are made over the telephone and it helps if you give your guests some details. If you invite a New Zealander for brunch, a combination of breakfast and lunch, they would expect a fairly substantial meal, probably with some cooked food. If it is lunch, around midday, it would be lighter fare, possibly a salad or soup in winter, and some sandwiches. The main meal in New Zealand is dinner, served around six to eight o'clock. Just to make things a bit more complicated, some people refer to it as 'tea'. 'Tea' is really tea when it is prefaced with either 'morning' or 'afternoon' when a short break is taken to drink a cup of tea or coffee. A friend of mine who immigrated to New Zealand from another English-speaking country was not aware of this distinction, and it got him into a rather embarrassing situation. After he had been in the country for some months, he decided to invite his boss and his wife for afternoon tea. He invited them for 'tea' and told them to come around four o'clock. The guests duly arrived and were served some tea and some cakes that they thoroughly enjoyed. And then they stayed, and stayed, and stayed. Around six o'clock my friend and his wife began to get a bit anxious. There was a hasty consultation in the kitchen, some meat was unfrozen and a salad was hastily prepared. "Would you like to stay for dinner? It will be quite simple, just a barbecue, " my friend asked his guests. "Well, er, yes please," they replied somewhat puzzled. After all, they had been invited to 'tea', which in New Zealand means an invitation for dinner.

The last meal of the day, often just a cup of tea or a snack, is supper. If you entertain guests for dinner, the visit usually concludes with supper. Just a cup of coffee or tea and some cakes are quite sufficient.

There are very few pitfalls when entertaining New Zealanders. You may like to ascertain that there is no food that they cannot eat for either religious or health reasons. They will certainly appreciate your hospitality, particularly if you can serve them some of your own culture's dishes.

ALL WORK AND NO PLAY

You may be in New Zealand to work, and a few words about workplace etiquette may be helpful. Fellow workers, workmates in Kiwi English, will almost always address each other by their first names. The work atmosphere is usually pretty relaxed.

In the first few weeks, your workmates will probably tease you a bit or send you on meaningless errands. This could be a problem for people from Asian cultures because of the possible loss of face. Usually it is just a bit of harmless fun and the best way to deal with it is to have a bit of a laugh at yourself with them. What they are really testing is whether you 'fit in'. It is some kind of humorous induction and often expresses a degree of affection as well. So try not to take offence; normally none is intended.

Depending on the business you work in, you will work an eight-hour day, Monday to Friday, with an hour off for lunch and two short breaks for morning and afternoon tea, sometimes called 'smoko', particularly in the manual trades. Tea is usually provided by the employer, but in most cases you will have to bring your own lunch or buy it from a nearby dairy or lunch bar. Don't forget that the main meal in New Zealand is in the evening, so lunch is usually a quick snack. There is also no lengthy siesta, as there is in some countries. Really large factories and businesses may have their own staff cafeteria for their employees.

If you are required to do shiftwork, a roster will be set. There are strict rules in law about how many breaks you should have, how long the shifts may be, and how much time off you must have.

If you are having problems settling in, if your workmates tease you too much or beyond what you are prepared to tolerate, you can discuss the matter with your superior and ask him or her to take steps to help. Freedom from harassment is one of your rights under New Zealand law. If the matter gets really serious and your employer cannot or will not help, you can ask the New Zealand Human Rights Commission to handle your complaint. Its website is listed in the *Resource Guide*.

Chapter Four

LIFE DOWN UNDER

WATCH YOUR LANGUAGE

When I first arrived in New Zealand, I had very little English indeed. I had not taken it at school and, apart from a few lessons before departing to New Zealand, I used a grammar book and a dictionary and the ship's library to learn as much as I could. The ship's library did not contain much that would interest a teenager, but it did have the complete set of the *Biggles* books. Biggles is a fictional World War II air ace, and his conversation is peppered with 'what ho', 'jolly good', 'roger', 'there's a good chap' and other very, very British English phrases that no Kiwi, and by now, probably no English person, would use these days.

95

My English therefore must have caused much amusement when we landed in Wellington. At first this did not matter very much, because I was pitched straight into haymaking and other farm work that did not need communication at a very high level. Once I went to school however, this began to change. I discovered to my dismay that I understood very little of what the teacher was saying, so taking notes in class was virtually impossible, since I had to concentrate so hard on grasping what the words meant that I could not distinguish between what was important and what was not. But worse was to come. When I went into the playground, I found that my classmates, while friendly enough, simply did not talk the kind of English that I had carefully acquired from the *Biggles* books, but they used words and phrases that I had never heard of and simply had no idea what they meant. The problem was exacerbated by the fact that some of the language used in the playground was not particularly refined, and on one occasion I rather shocked the wife of one of my teachers by using a swearword without knowing that it was one.

I particularly remember one occasion when I had been invited to the home of one of my new friends. They were telling me some invented story about New Zealand customs (in New Zealand English, they were 'spinning me a yarn'!), when the mother of the friend in whose house we were said to me: "Don't let them pull your leg, Peter!" I looked down at both my legs, but neither of them was being pulled by anyone. Fortunately, I was young and was fairly quick on the uptake (another colloquialism, it means: 'I understood very quickly'), and it did not take me long to work out that what she meant was 'Don't let them tell you a pack of good humoured lies.'

Nowadays, technology can provide some assistance. Instead of having to carry a large and heavy dictionary with you, you can now buy an electronic dictionary that weighs a few grams and contains many words at an electronic goods store. It still will not help you with local slang though.

If you are reading this book it means that you have at least enough English to read it. Congratulations! Because if you or one of your family members does not have a reasonably good grasp of the language, the whole process of settling in is going to take much longer and would be more difficult. I would certainly strongly encourage non-English speakers contemplating living in New Zealand for some time to learn as much English as they can, both before setting out and, if necessary, once they get here.

Kiwi Slang

But the task does not end with you having achieved a high level of English, because English may have a common basic structure and vocabulary, but there are a myriad of different local variations. For example, you may have diligently learned all your words when you learned the language, but what would you do if someone at a party asked you where the loo was? 'Loo' is the word New Zealanders use for toilet, or what the Americans call 'restroom'. (I cannot for the life of me fathom why. If I want to go for a rest, a men's urinal would be the last place I would choose!) At the same party, you may be served a 'banger' or a 'snarler'. Don't worry, it will not make a sudden noise or snarl at you. In fact, it is perfectly edible: it is simply a sausage. But if you like it, you may tell your host that you think it is 'cracker', which means 'very good indeed'. You may well get something alcoholic to drink with your 'bangers', and if the party is not very high class, you may hear that referred to as 'piss'. While this word originally means urine, it is used for any alcohol, except in phrases like 'piss around' which means, 'wasting time'. Just be careful that you don't 'get pissed' (drunk), because if you do, your hosts or your partner may get 'pissed off'(angry or upset).

Obviously, I cannot provide you with a complete list of New Zealand slang. There is a partial list (with translations into US English) on the Internet and I have listed the website in the *Resource*

Guide. But you can consider yourself proficient in New Zealand slang if you can translate the following:

Last Sunday we took the old bomb up into the wop-wops to a place where my parents used to have a bach. I had forgotten the way, and we did a bit of a tiki tour because a cockie put us crook. But then we asked another joker whose directions were spot on and once we found the right road, we had it sussed. By the time we thought of going home it had got a bit late, so we had to rattle our dags. We did not feel like cooking dinner so we took home some shark and greasies and had them with a couple of stubbies.

And here is the translation:

Last Sunday we took the very old, and not very well maintained, car into a remote part of the country where my parents used to have a holiday home. I had forgotten the way, and we drove around a bit because a farmer gave us the wrong information. But then we asked another person whose directions were exactly right and once we found the right road we had figured it out. By the time we thought of going home, it had got a bit late, so we had to hurry up. We did not feel like cooking dinner so we took home some fish and chips and had them with a couple of small bottles of beer.

I hope that you don't find this too discouraging. It won't take you long to learn New Zealand speak; it is mainly English, and when a Kiwi says to you: "Good on yer mate!" this is not inappropriate familiarity, he is simply bestowing on you the highest seal of approval for something you have said or done.

Finally, you may be invited to a social function, like we were when we first came to New Zealand. "We are not going to a lot of trouble with the food," the hostess said when she rang to invite us, "just bring a plate." We arrived with an empty plate and then discovered, to our embarrassment, that all the other Kiwi guests had brought a plate filled with some finger food. We never made that mistake again. If you are invited and asked to 'bring a plate', it means that you are asked to make a contribution to the food.

GETTING AROUND

Kiwis love their cars. The 3.8 million men, women and children own, between them, 2.3 million vehicles. On a per capita basis, New Zealand has the second highest rate of car ownership in the world. The Kiwi bird lost its ability to fly because it did not need to use its wings. I would not be surprised if the human Kiwis will soon lose their ability to walk. I had a colleague at university who regularly used his car to drive right around the campus to a building that he could have reached by walking on a very pleasant paved path in three minutes.

When I arrived in New Zealand, Kiwis were driving mainly British, American and Australian cars. This has now changed and the New Zealand streets are dominated by Japanese cars. British cars, apart from luxury models such as a Jaguar and Rover which make a small segment of the market, have virtually disappeared. Toyota, Mazda and Mitsubishi have taken over. A feature of the New Zealand car market recently has been the large scale import of second-hand cars from Japan. Since the Japanese also drive on the left side of the road, they can be driven here without any modification.

Auckland city traffic during the day. The Sky Tower is in the background. The Sky Tower is the tallest structure in the Southern Hemisphere.

Knowing the Roads

New Zealand has a very good network of roads, although there are only short stretches of motorway around the major cities. All major roads are paved, and you can drive from Kaitaia in the north of the North Island to Invercargill in the south of the South Island without having to drive on unsealed roads. There are still plenty of them, but they are in remote areas. To get to the real 'backblocks' of New Zealand (the 'wop-wops' we have just learned about!), you will still have to brave unsealed, often dusty roads, but to me that is a small price to pay for one of my favourite pastimes; visiting remote parts of this beautiful country.

Last year, I was in Beijing and needed a taxi to get from my appointment back to my hotel. When I got in, I automatically reached for the seatbelt and clicked it shut. The driver got upset and angry because he thought I had put on the belt because I did not trust his driving. My action had nothing to do with that, although Beijing traffic can be pretty exciting. It was simply a habit because in New Zealand, you can be fined if you don't wear a seatbelt both in the front and in the back seat. If you are the driver of a car it is your duty to ensure that all your passengers are securely belted in and that any child under five years old is in a safety-approved child seat.

The speed limit for cars in New Zealand is generally 100km/h (62mph) on the open road and 50km/h (31mph) in built up areas. Other legal limits (for example 80 km/h zones) are clearly marked on roadside signs which are white disks with a red border. When you approach corners, there are often also yellow signs that indicate the speed at which you can safely negotiate the bend. These are not legal limits, and if you go faster, you will not get fined. If you go much faster, however, you may run off the road and end up in a ditch!

New Zealand roads have recently acquired another sign which is brown in colour and will direct drivers to scenic spots or amenities. Again, these are meant to be helpful rather than pointing out some legal requirement.

Not so clearly marked are speed cameras that are situated in police vans along the roadside. They will take your photo and indicate the speed you were doing when the photo was taken. If you are caught, you will get a speed infringement notice and you have a choice of either paying the fine or going to court to have your case heard. A friend of mine had the misfortune to be caught on a speed camera photo exceeding the speed limit. He wrote to the police and requested a copy of the photo (to which you are entitled). After he had received it, he wrote a cheque for the amount of the fine, took a photo of the cheque and posted it off to the police. After about ten days, he received his reply: a photo of a pair of handcuffs!

Some police cars, both marked and unmarked, are fitted with radar speed devices that can register your speed no matter what direction you are travelling in. If you are over the speed limit and caught, you will be pursued by the police car. It will use its flashing lights and, possibly, its siren, to alert you to the fact that you must stop as soon as possible. Pull over to the side of the road as soon as it is safe to do so. If you get caught in this way, you may be fined up to NZ$1000 and, in addition, be slapped with demerit points. If you get more than 100 demerit points in any one year, your licence will be suspended for three months. The fine for general motor offences can range between NZ$2000 and NZ$20,000. The fine for speeding can be as high as NZ$630 if you are caught driving 50km/h above the speed limit. The police can also fine you NZ$150 for not wearing a seatbelt. For higher speeds and more serious offences, the police will take you to court where the penalties are, of course, higher.

Licences, Drivers and Car Insurance

If you want to drive a car in New Zealand, you must have a drivers licence from your home country and an international driving permit. This will allow you to drive here for up to one year. After that, you will have to apply for a New Zealand licence and pass a practical and a written test on the New Zealand Road Code. If you meet certain criteria and come from Australia, Canada, Norway, the European Union, South Africa, Switzerland or the United States, you may apply for exemption from the practical test. This applies to licences for private cars only. If you would like to drive a motorcycle, truck, bus or taxi, you will need to get a special licence. Obviously, there will be a cost involved. In every case however, I would suggest that you should get yourself a copy of the official New Zealand Road Code and become familiar with the rules that govern driving on New Zealand roads. With the increasing number of international tourists, there are accidents that involve tourists. Analysis has revealed that, in some cases, it was simply ignorance of New Zealand road rules that has led to such accidents. The New Zealand Road Code is available from all major bookshops.

Driving in New Zealand is comparatively easy because traffic is light outside the major cities. New Zealand city traffic is relatively orderly. Every now and again, there are articles or readers' letters in the local newspapers deploring the fact that New Zealand drivers are terrible compared with drivers in other parts of the world. Of course, there are some terrible drivers in New Zealand, but as far as I can see, they are in about the same proportions as elsewhere. It is true that they tend to lack experience with driving in heavy traffic, but how can they get that experience when normal traffic is simply not heavy!

If you intend to drive a car in New Zealand (and you will see from the rest of this section, it is almost a necessity if you want to get around), I would suggest that you consider joining the Automobile Association (AA). They not only provide a breakdown service, they also will, for a small fee, inspect any car you intend to buy, and supply you with good maps, accommodation guides and itineraries when you want to drive around the country.

If you buy a car, it is very important that you also get car insurance. If you are not insured and have a crash, you may be liable for all costs and risk having to pay large amounts of money. So getting insurance is a wise precaution. Insurance companies are listed in the Yellow Pages of the telephone directory, and they will be able to advise you on different types of cover and costs.

Beware of the Cows

One of the hazards you may encounter while driving in New Zealand, particularly on country roads, are herds of cows and flocks of sheep that are driven along the road. The best way to deal with them is simply to pull over and wait for them to pass. Cows, in particular, have a habit of looking at the car in amazement, but not moving aside, so you will just have to be patient. Some time ago, I was sitting in the front seat of a bus beside the driver. As we rounded a bend, there was a huge flock of sheep. We were carefully picking our way through them when a speeding motorcycle suddenly approached from the other side of the bend. The rider put on his brakes hard, flew over the handlebars, rolled and bounced over the woolly sheep and landed on the road. He was a bit dazed, but completely uninjured.

He was lucky! When driving in the country at night, you have to take particular care. A friend of mine collided one dark night with a stray cow. My friend was badly injured and had to spend several weeks in hospital.

Farmers whose stock has to cross the road regularly for milking on busier regional roads will have a warning sign and flashing lights to ensure the safety of their stock and the drivers. If you see such a sign, slow down immediately and proceed with caution. The first cows may just be entering the crossing as you approach.

Getting around the country without a car is rather more cumbersome. New Zealand air services are quite comprehensive, not only just to the major cities, but also to a good number of provincial towns. The fares vary on the main routes , depending on when you fly, how far ahead you book, and where you book (you can get discounted rates for booking on the Internet). So it pays to plan ahead and make some inquiries about fares.

City buses are not very frequent.

Public Buses

Public bus services span the entire country, but because of the low population density and the high use of private cars, they are not very frequent. A colleague of mine from a country with an efficient and frequent public transport system found out about this to his cost. He was travelling in the South Island and had just arrived at lunchtime on a Friday in a picturesque town on the western coast. The connecting bus that was to take him to the next tourist spot was waiting to leave as he arrived, but he decided that this little town was such a delightful spot that he would have a cup of coffee, relax a bit and then take the next bus to his final destination for the day. So he let the first bus go and had a leisurely lunch. He then asked at what time the next bus would leave for his destination; "11 a.m. on Monday," came the reply. So my friend was stuck for the weekend, and the little town lost some of its charm by the time he was finally able to escape it.

You will find that there are usually several buses daily between major cities, but only one service per day (and sometimes not even every day) between smaller centres. Timetables are not easy to find, and, at times, there are no printed timetables. The way to find out is to go to the Yellow Pages of your local telephone directory and look under 'Bus Charters & Services'. There, you will find the telephone numbers of various bus companies and the towns they serve. For bus services within a city (and only larger cities have them), you generally can get a printed timetable from the Citizens Advice Bureau or the bus company. Don't expect a frequent service though. Kiwis, as I have said, love their cars.

Trains

This love of cars has also affected long distance train services. These have been pruned back and back and back, so that now you can travel by train only between Auckland and Wellington (one daytrain and one overnight train), Picton, at the top of the South Island, to Christchurch (one train in each direction per day), and on a tourist excursion train from Christchurch across the Southern Alps to Greymouth (one return journey per day). I would recommend you do a trip or two simply for their touristic value, as long as you don't mind the slowness of the trip and the ancient rolling stock. The routes are indeed scenic, and you see parts of the country that you don't see if you have to drive yourself. Apart from that however, you are better off taking a bus or your car. You will, incidentally, not be able to take a passenger train to the world's southernmost railway station, which is in New Zealand, at the bottom of the South Island. Only freight trains call there now.

Apart from the long-haul operations, there are basic suburban rail services in Wellington and Auckland taking commuters from the suburbs into the central business district. There are efforts at the moment to upgrade and increase suburban rail services in Auckland to alleviate the increasing congestion on the city's roads.

In addition to scheduled bus and rail services there is, of course, a large range of package tours by road or rail, ranging from a few days to several weeks. While they are patronised mainly by overseas tourists, New Zealanders also make use of them to see the scenic spots of their own country.

Ferries

When I wrote about the New Zealand road system, I said that you could drive from Kaitaia to Invercargill on sealed roads. Did you notice the deliberate mistake? It is called Cook Strait: 30 km (19 miles) of often-very-turbulent sea that separates the North from the South Island. There are two companies that provide ferry services across Cook Strait; from Wellington to Picton. Timetables are available on their websites listed in the *Resource Guide*. The ferries transport passengers, cars, trucks and even freight trains. The crossing takes about three and a half hours on the conventional ferries, and since a good proportion of the journey is through Queen Charlotte sound, there is plenty of lovely scenery to admire. It would be advisable to book ahead during the school holidays and summer breaks when traffic is heavy.

GETTING WHAT YOU NEED

Unless you live way out in a remote country region, from where a drive to the shops can take several hours, you will not have much trouble getting the necessities of life at almost any time of the day or night. Shops are open most days of the year, but you will find that outside tourist centres, the majority of shops will be closed on Christmas Day, Good Friday, Easter Sunday and on the morning of Anzac Day. Hours of opening are generally from 9 a.m. to 5:30 p.m. Monday to Friday, and 9:00 a.m. to 12:00 noon on Saturday, but retailers have the flexibility to choose their daily operating hours. Supermarkets open earlier and close later, and they usually display their hours of opening on a notice at their doors. Supermarkets and

107

shopping malls in larger cities will also open on Sunday, and some of the busiest ones now open for 24 hours.

Consumer goods are freely available, and most world brands are stocked by speciality shops. Not too many years ago, immigrants to New Zealand, particularly if they came from Europe, felt that they were coming to the end of the earth. They brought their own refrigerators and washing machines because they feared that they would not be able to get these items here or that they would be of inferior quality. One immigrant from Europe even brought a prefabricated house! You can get all these things here; they are of very good quality, and if you need a new part for your New Zealand-made refrigerator, you can get it within minutes, while it could be almost impossible to source a part or a knowledgeable technician for your fancy European or American machine.

A shopping mall consists of dozens of independent stores under one roof.

Supermarkets, Dairies and Petrol Stations

For food and everyday needs most Kiwis now go to the supermarket. It has the greatest variety and generally the lowest prices. Unlike in supermarkets in some countries I have visited and lived in, New Zealand checkout operators will actually greet you, often with a smile, no matter how long the queue is. I tend to smile back and exchange a few words with them as they put the groceries across the barcode reader or weigh the bananas. It makes shopping so much more pleasant.

What makes it pleasant is, of course, the brief human contact, something that in the past used to keep you shopping with the family grocer for year after year after year. New Zealand, for many decades, had dairies, fairly small shops that sold milk and milk products as well as a variety of groceries, sweets, cigarettes, ice cream and newspapers. They were open when all the other shops were closed and provided a service as well as the personal touch. There are still some about, but in the face of competition from supermarkets and service stations, there are fewer every year.

The corner dairy sells basic groceries, but the service is warm and personal.

If you have forgotten something or suddenly feel like a midnight snack and the supermarket is closed and there is no dairy close by, don't despair. Many petrol stations have turned into mini supermarkets in the last few years, and some of them are open 24 hours.

Discounts and Taxes

On the whole, New Zealanders don't bargain and pay the advertised price without a murmur. With some large purchases, you may get a discount of some kind if you ask for it, particularly, if the item is subject to fierce competition and you are prepared to pay with cash. Some shops will also lower the price if you can prove that it is sold cheaper at another shop. The advertised price, incidentally, almost invariably includes the Goods and Services Tax (GST). It pays to check however, particularly in the field of computers and consumer electronics, where the words '+GST' behind the price mean that you will have to add 12.5% to the advertised price. I am always a little irritated when I travel in the United States, where the advertised price is never the price you actually pay because taxes get added once you have decided to buy. In New Zealand, you pay what the sticker says (unless, of course, you have managed to negotiate a discount).

In some cases, where you buy larger household appliances, the shop may take your old appliance, if you have one, as a 'trade-in'. This means that they will give you a certain sum of money for it. These trade-in deals are often advertised for a limited period in the local press, so keep an eye on the advertisements. You may also want to use time payment, called 'hire purchase' in New Zealand, for larger items. Make sure that you check carefully how much extra you pay by way of interest, finance and other charges. Again, special deals are often advertised in the daily paper where you may be able to pay off an item with no interest being charged for several months. If you shop around, you can often get some good deals, but make sure you do your sums carefully.

Roadside Stands

Apart from the fruit and vegetable shops in the cities and the supermarkets, you will find roadside sales of fresh produce along stretches of roads where there are market gardens and orchards. The shops range from small stalls, often unattended, with a tin into which you put your payment, to huge barns that sell the products of the enterprise and a whole lot more, such as honey from an apiary nearby, home-made chocolate, and even frozen goods and soft drinks. Some of the berry gardens will sell you their berries in tinfoil or plastic punnets. For a reduced price, they will hand you an empty punnet and let you pick your own. They usually advertise this with big 'Pick your Own' signs by the road.

Fresh produce can be bought along shopping streets.

Ethnic Shops

One of the pleasures of shopping for some groups of expatriates is having an ethnic shop nearby. I am fortunate to have a Dutch-owned shop within walking distance of my home where I can buy a whole range of products that I could get when I lived in Europe. They also make their own cheese, which is just as good, if not better, than what could be bought in Holland. There are many speciality food shops throughout New Zealand. Just inquire from someone of your culture who has lived here for a while.

Pills and Plants

If you need any healthcare products and cosmetics, you would go to a pharmacy in many English-speaking countries. In New Zealand, you go to the chemist. Chemists are also registered to dispense prescription medicines, so if your doctor prescribes some drugs, you will have to go to the chemist to get them. You may find that a much wider range of drugs is subject to prescription in New Zealand than in many other countries.

Plants, trees and shrubs for your garden are often sold in the gardening section of your supermarket. You will also find garden centres on the outskirts of the town or city in which you live. They generally have a wider range of stock than the supermarket centres. Staff in the garden centres, both in the supermarket and in the larger ones, are usually enthusiasts and are very happy to chat and advise you. I have often received helpful tips from them and have never regretted acting according to their advice.

Post Offices

You may be surprised to find that there are no longer any of the old-fashioned post offices in New Zealand. While there is, of course, a postal service—New Zealand Post—the customer interface is now in 'Post Shops', which are often stationery and magazine shops that have one or two postal counters. Letters can be mailed locally in either of two classes: Standard Post, which means that they will arrive at their destination on the next day within the town in which they were posted or within two to three working days nationwide; and FastPost, where letters will arrive on the next day if you are sending it between major towns and cities. When posting a letter, make sure that you pick the right letterbox. Standard Post and FastPost letters are posted in separate boxes. International letters and parcels can be sent by International Express, International Air or International Economy. Postage rates are listed on the NZ Post website which you can find in the *Resource Guide*, or else you can ask at the local Post Shop.

GETTING FED AND WATERED

Not very many years ago, I had to drive a foreign VIP from Hamilton to Auckland. As we were driving through a small country town around lunchtime, he suddenly felt the pangs of hunger and insisted that we stop there and then for lunch. I was rather dubious, but he pointed to a sign that said 'Restaurant' above the entrance to what was a fish shop. It had a back room that contained some rickety tubular-steel chairs and four formica topped tables decorated with plastic flowers and Coca-Cola bottles filled with tomato sauce. The proprietor handed us the greasy menu laminated in plastic, which offered mainly fish with chips (French fries, if you are from the United States), egg (fried), and tomato (fried). If you did not like fish, you could have steak with chips, egg (fried), and tomato (fried). We ordered the fish with chips. After a while, the meals arrived; huge fish fillets overhung the sides of a very large plate (and by doing so, hid the black-rimmed thumbnail of the proprietor placing it on the table). The fillets were flanked by a mountain of chips and decorated with a tiny sprig of parsley. My guest asked whether he could have some lemon with the fish. The proprietor withdrew, and I heard him call one of his children. Soon after, a little boy sprinted out of the shop, ran to the fruit stall up the road and returned with a lemon, which was then cut in half in the kitchen, placed on a saucer and brought to us with great ceremony. The fish, incidentally, was very fresh and delicious.

New Zealand gastronomy has come a long way since then. Not just in tourist centres, but also in most larger cities, will you find an exciting café and restaurant culture. In a 300-metre (90-foot) stretch

A lunch bar in an industrial area.

of the main street of my home city of Hamilton, I can now eat Turkish, Chinese, Japanese, Thai, Italian, American and New Zealand food, or I can sit at a table on the footpath outside three different cafés, sipping my latte while the world goes by. And this is not only the case in my home city. Wellington is not only the most southerly national capital in the world, it now also boasts more restaurants per head of population than—wait for it—New York City!

As in other parts of the world, the prices vary, but on the whole my impression is that the quality/price ratio has improved with increased competition, so that unless you simply want to go to an exclusive restaurant and pay accordingly, you can get some very good meals at very reasonable prices.

When you order in a New Zealand restaurant, you will be handed a menu that is normally subdivided into 'starters', 'entrées', 'main courses' and 'desserts'. You do not have to order from each category. I usually have either a starter or an entrée, but not both, and I almost always skip dessert and have a cup of coffee instead. The important thing to be aware of is that, as in other Western restaurants, you order only one dish from each category. My Malaysian brother-in-law tells the story of how he and a friend travelled to New Zealand to take up scholarships. They had never been outside Malaysia before and were used to Chinese restaurants. En route, they had to spend a night in a hotel. After they had scrutinized the menu in the dining room, they proceeded to order a whole number of dishes, as was their custom at home. The waiter politely asked whether they really wanted all these dishes. "Oh yes, we do," they replied. Before long they found themselves inundated with much more food than they could possibly eat. I think that they made the mistake only once.

Many restaurants in New Zealand will display the sign 'Fully Licensed', which means that they are licensed to serve alcohol. If they have a BYO (Bring Your Own) licence, you may bring your own alcohol (generally only wine or beer), and they will serve it for you but will charge a small 'corkage' fee.

Numerous sidewalk cafés can be found in Auckland.

If your taste is for the simpler fare of chain restaurants, you will also be well served in New Zealand. All the major U.S. chains, from Burger King to McDonalds, KFC, and Pizza Hut have outlets all over the country, so you will not be deprived of the products of the globalized fast food industry.

Food is also available in the shopping malls that have proliferated in the New Zealand towns over the last couple of decades. Most of them have a 'food hall', where you can get fairly cheap meals ranging from the ubiquitous Chinese smorgasbord to Indian tandoori and Italian pizza and pasta, with almost everything in between. And then there are, of course, the numerous Chinese 'Take Away' bars that sell Westernised as well as authentic Chinese food for you to take away in plastic containers. Of course, you can always find the good old traditional fish and chips shops. Fried fish and chips is the original takeaway meal. Originally imported from Britain, I think it tastes much better here in New Zealand because, unlike in many places in Britain, it is always freshly made for you while you wait. This is a treat that is bad for your blood cholesterol level (which can lead to heart disease) but oh-so-yummy!

If you buy food from one of the chains or takeaway places I have just mentioned, or from one of the numerous coffee bars that serve sandwiches, muffins, sausage rolls and pies for lunch, you pay as you order. In the restaurants that have more elaborate menus, you usually pay at the end of the meal at the cash desk by the exit. There was a time when tipping was not acceptable in New Zealand. Unfortunately, in my view, American and European tourists are bringing the custom into the country. Tips are still not expected, but most waiting personnel will now take them, even though they are paid perfectly adequate money for doing their job. While I tip when I visit countries where I know that waiters and waitresses depend on tips for a decent wage, I do not tip in New Zealand, but I will smile and say thank you if I get good service.

The Maori Hangi

New Zealand cuisine is fairly international. The only famous indigenous dish is the Maori *hangi*, which is meat (mainly pork and mutton) and root vegetables (potatoes, *kumara*, pumpkin) cooked in an earth oven. Putting down a *hangi* is quite a complex procedure. First, a pit is dug. This is the earth oven or *umu*. It needs to be deep enough for the food, depending on the catered number of people. Then fist-sized stones, often *hangi* stones, are heated on a large fire built beside the pit. (*Hangi* stones do not explode when heated). There must be enough stones to line the bottom of the pit. When the stones are white hot—a process that takes about three to four hours—they are raked into the pit. Wire baskets filled with wrapped food are placed on top of the stones and covered with wet tea towels and sacks. Traditionally, the food was wrapped in leaves, but nowadays, tinfoil is used as a convenient replacement. Water is sloshed over the food

117

to create steam, and the earth is shovelled back onto the covered food until no more steam escapes. The cooking phase is a lengthy one; three and a half to four hours are required for the food to cook properly. Apparently, it is virtually impossible to overcook a *hangi*, and most of the failures result from digging it up too early. Opening the oven is comparatively simple, as long as you are careful not to get too much dirt onto the wire basket and the food. Given the time it takes to prepare the oven and heat the stones as well as the cooking time, you will need to start at about 9:00 a.m. if you want to serve the *hangi* at about 6:00 p.m., but believe me, the delicious food that comes out of a well prepared *hangi* is worth the wait.

Pies and Grub

The other famous culinary treat for Kiwis is the good old New Zealand pie, a small round pie filled with (often gristly) bits of steak in a gravy, or fatty beef mince encased in pastry. It is an acquired taste and almost impossible to eat politely with your fingers, since the hot gravy will inevitably run down over your hand as you bite into it and crumbs from the crust will get all over your clothes. Our nutrition experts also tell us that pies are not good for us because they contain too much fat. Having said all that, I have to confess that once every week or three, I indulge in a good old New Zealand pie for lunch—and I love every bit of it!

Perhaps it is a sign of the increasing sophistication of the New Zealand food industry that in recent times, the humble pie has become a gourmet item. Apart from the traditional mince and steak pie, you can now buy chicken pies, lamb pies and even venison pies. There is also an annual competition for bakers to produce the best pie in New Zealand. This attracts hundreds of entries. (The judges must be thoroughly sick of pies by the time the judging is finished.)

If you have really exotic tastes in food you may want to attend one of the wildfoods festivals. Perhaps the most famous is held in Hokitika in March. There, you can try delicacies like *huhu* grubs (a honey coloured grub that lives in decaying trees), Westcargots (west coast snails cooked in wine), gumboot milkshakes, high-protein earthworms, whisky sausages or bambi burgers.

New Zealand Cooking—How To?

If you do not want to eat prepared food all the time, then you obviously have to cook your own meals. I have already pointed out that it is quite easy to find shops selling ingredients for European or Asian cooking. But what about wholesome, plain, if somewhat stodgy, New Zealand cooking? I'm pleased to say that you are in luck if you are looking for a New Zealand cookbook and I recommend the *Edmond's Cookery Book*. It is sold in bookshops and in most supermarkets. While there are plenty of New Zealand gourmet cookbooks, this is the guide to simple, everyday, New Zealand cooking and baking. It was first published in 1907 and by now has sold more than 3 million copies. This makes it not only the biggest-selling cookbook in New Zealand, but the best-selling book ever published in New Zealand! In it, you will find instructions to cook simple meals, stews, vegetable dishes,

A New Zealand favourite—fish and chips.

119

cakes and biscuits. *Edmond's Cookery Book* has become an icon in New Zealand. It is even used outside New Zealand as well. My sister's housemaid in Kuching, Sarawak, was given one and uses it to cook for her part-time catering business. This means that if there is a social occasion in one of the villages in and around Kuching and she does the catering, the Malaysian guests will be eating chocolate cake and Anzac biscuits made to recipes from *Edmond's Cookery Book.*

Drinking Water

If all this talk of food has made you thirsty, I should perhaps say a few words about drink. New Zealand tap water is drinkable anywhere in the country and conforms to strict health standards. Of late, it has become fashionable here to drink bottled water, but I for one cannot see the need for it. I recently entertained a group of Chinese officials in my room at the university. Somehow the talk came around to the quality of drinking water, and I made the point about our tap water being drinkable. As I was escorting them out of the building at the end of the interview, they passed a large plastic cylinder filled with water and a stack of paper cups beside it. "Ah, pounced one of them. Caught you out! You need to purify your water!" The container was, in fact, a water cooler that was filled every morning—from the tap!

Not all New Zealanders enjoy piped water from a central supply. Farmhouses often have to rely on borehole water. We had such a borehole on the farm that was our first home in New Zealand. There are two problems with having your own borehole. Firstly, the pump that supplies your house and milking shed is driven by an electric motor. If there is a power cut (a rare occurrence in New Zealand compared with other parts of the world, but it does happen from time to time), you not only have no electricity, you also have no water once the header tank is exhausted. The second problem is that the pump can break down. Again, this does not happen very often, but for some reason, water pumps seem to know when it is Sunday or a public holiday, and they invariably choose to break down on these days when it is impossible to get a service mechanic to come out to the often remote farm and fix it. Thank goodness for the Number-8-wire mentality. My father and I spent many happy hours some Sundays wielding spanners and screwdrivers coaxing just a little bit more life out of our elderly water pump.

In areas where borehole water is not available, rainwater is used. A large concrete water tank is set up beside the house, and the rainwater that drains off the roof is piped into the tank where it is stored. This works fine as long as there is enough rain. In very dry summer, this can lead to water shortages. I well remember looking after a friend's sheep farm one summer and keeping an anxious eye on the tank gauge.

One of the disadvantages of borehole water and rainwater is that it is not fluoridated, as are most of the town water supplies. If you want to have the fluoride most town dwellers get automatically, you will have to get fluoride tablets. Some town supplies also are not fluoridated, so it pays to check and buy the tablets if you want them. And yes, you buy them from the chemist.

Alcohol

If water is not to your taste, you may prefer beer. Many New Zealanders do; they drink about 80 litres (21 gallons) per capita, which equates to a total annual production of 307 million litres (81 million gallons), so there should be some left for you. One of New Zealand's best-kept secrets is its wine. The early settlers brought vines with them which grew and thrived in the New Zealand soil and climate. It is however, only in the last 30 to 40 years that New Zealand wines have caught international attention. If you like wine and have not yet tried some of the New Zealand wines, you have a treat in store for you.

As a result of the rise of the wine industry, a whole wine culture is developing in New Zealand. Many, if not most, wineries have now restaurants attached to them where you can get a meal and sample the local product. If you like it, you can buy a case or two to take home. Since many wineries are out in the country, the setting of these restaurants is often very beautiful. A visit and a meal in beautiful surroundings add up to a very pleasant experience. A few years ago, my wife and I spent a night in Gisborne on the east coast of the North Island. We found that an old wharf shed at the port had been turned into a wine restaurant. We spent a very pleasant couple of hours sitting at the wharf's edge, sampling the (excellent) local wines and watching the fishermen unloading their catch while the sun was slowly setting. It was a truly memorable evening.

You can buy wine and beer at the supermarket, but not spirits. For those you will have to go to a liquor store. Just for your interest; the *Pakeha* pioneer forefathers in New Zealand drank an awful lot more spirits than the present-day Kiwis. Per capita consumption of spirits in 1886 was more than twice as much as that today.

GETTING INFORMED AND ENTERTAINED

New Zealanders are great readers. Indeed, a recent survey showed that reading was one of the country's top leisure activities, and New Zealand has the highest number of book stores per capita in the world. It is therefore not surprising that in relation to its population, New Zealand has a high number of daily newspapers; 26 of them. There are also two Sunday papers and around 120 local community newspapers. I have noticed that at the entrance to some supermarkets, free Chinese newspapers are also available.

One of the features of the New Zealand press is its good coverage of international news. Even provincial dailies will carry extensive news from outside New Zealand. Being geographically isolated, New Zealanders tend to make a greater effort to be informed about what goes on in the rest of the world.

To cater to the reading public, New Zealand has a good network of public libraries. While there often is a small charge for specialist collections or services, the general collection is usually free. If you want to join, you must be a resident of the town or city in which the library is located. The librarian who issues you with the borrower's card will ask you to provide some proof that you are a resident (e.g. a bank statement addressed to you). If you would like to learn English by listening, you can get a 'talking book' in some libraries for a small fee. A 'talking book' is a book read and recorded on cassette tape or CD. You can, of course, also buy 'talking books' in bookshops. They can be a great aid to learning to comprehend spoken English. You can even 'read' them while driving!

Museums

For a young country, New Zealand has a lot of history, or, perhaps, its comparatively short history has been well documented. The New Zealand Museums website lists all the museums and art galleries found in New Zealand. There are more than 300 of them, which is quite a respectable number for a country of just under four million people. The museums range in size and quality. The Auckland Museum, known in Auckland as the War Memorial Museum because it is also Auckland's war memorial, is one of the largest museums in the country. The Te Papa Tongarewa (Museum of New Zealand) has an impressive way of making history come alive through sound, light and interactive displays.

There are, of course, a multitude of small local museums and some quaint specialist collections. If you ever get to Whangarei, you may find Claphams Clocks—a museum devoted entirely to clocks—quite interesting. On the western coast of the South Island, you will find the Shantytown Museum, a reconstruction of a gold mining town of the late 19th century where you can even have a go at panning gold. If you enjoy vintage railways, there is an old steam train operating at Glenbrook, just southwest of Auckland, and another, the Kingston Flyer, on the southern shore of Lake Whakatipu in the South Island. But as I have said, there are many museums and art galleries in New Zealand, and if you drive through a city or in the countryside and see a signpost marked 'Museum', you will almost always find something of interest if you take the trouble to visit.

Telephone Directories

Your local telephone directory is an amazingly versatile source of information. In addition to the Yellow Pages that give you information about businesses and services, there is a section at the beginning of the White Pages that gives you all the services offered by New Zealand Telecom. Another set of pages—called the Blue Pages— gives you all the local and national government agencies. You can also find all registered medical practitioners (doctors), medical centres and hospitals in the area covered by the directory. The number that is used to access emergency services in New Zealand is 111. There is the story of old Trevor whose wife died one evening. He rang 111 and the operator told him that she would send someone over straight away. She asked him where he lived and he told her that he lived at the end of Eucalyptus Drive. "Can you spell that for me please?" said the operator. There was a long pause and then Trevor said, "How about I drag her over to Oak Street and you pick her up there?"

Radio, Television and Film

The radio has a mixture of publicly-funded stations and private commercial stations catering to virtually every taste; from classical music to pop, sports coverage and around-the-clock talkback. Television is available throughout the country, with two publicly-owned and two private free-to-air channels plus one major pay TV provider, Sky, which gives you access to international channels like Discovery, BBC and CNN.

One of the features of New Zealand television that I personally find annoying is the high proportion of time that is devoted to commercial advertising. The reason for this is that the publicly-owned channels are required to be run as a business and therefore must generate their own income. To find information about programmes, the daily newspapers have listings. There are also magazines such as *The Listener*, or *The TV Guide* that can be bought at supermarkets, book stores or dairies. They have more detailed listings and usually cover a week's worth of programming.

If you want to go out to be entertained, there is a state-subsidised symphony orchestra and the Royal New Zealand Ballet (both of which tour the country regularly), as well as a lively film industry. The *Lord of the Rings* trilogy was filmed in New Zealand and directed by Kiwi Peter Jackson. Did you also know that almost 150 feature films were made in New Zealand since 1977? This includes the recent Hollywood production *The Last Samurai*. Information on filming in New Zealand can be found on the website for Film New Zealand, which is listed in the *Resource Guide*.

Night Life

For many people, a popular evening's entertainment is going to the pub. While I do not visit pubs frequently, I have found that often different pubs cater to different patron groups. There are pubs that are visited mainly by young people, where live bands or recorded music make it necessary for you to shout into your neighbour's ear if you want to be understood, and there are quieter bars which I personally find more congenial. Many country pubs (they are invariable called 'hotels' even though their main purpose is to serve alcohol, not to provide accommodation), have a 'Public Bar', which is usually the noisier of the two, and a 'Lounge Bar', which is quieter and a little bit more refined. In the old days, women would not go to the public bar but would sit primly in the lounge bar, sipping their Pimm's Cup (a rather obscure English liqueur) or sweet sherry. This has now changed, as has the whole public drinking scene. When I first came to New Zealand, the first 'beer gardens' were just beginning to appear in New Zealand pubs. They were screened off with high fences from public view because patrons were not permitted to be seen by the public drinking beer. Nowadays, I can sit outside a restaurant at tables set out on the public footpath and watch people pass while enjoying a beer.

In the course of the general liberalisation of public entertainment, and spurred on by the growing tourist trade, New Zealand has also acquired a number of nightclubs in the major cities and tourist centres. I must confess that I have never been to one, but my students who claim to have some expertise in such matters, assure me that they are up to 'international standards', that is, the entertainment, the acts, the music, and presumably the prices, are the same as you would find in any part of the world.

Being Part of the Entertainment

Your city or town most probably will have an amateur live drama theatre or society. They will advertise for people to audition for parts in their productions. Perhaps they can entice you to take the plunge and show off your talents. If you sing or play a musical instrument, New Zealand cities and country towns have a whole lot of amateur choirs and orchestras. Some of the choirs are very good, having won international competitions, and admission to the better ones is by audition. As always, check with your local Citizens Advice Bureau and if you are interested, do the New Zealand thing: 'give it a go'. You will not only enjoy it, you may even make a few new friends.

By now we have you settled into New Zealand, fed, watered and entertained. But life is not just fun and games. Perhaps we should now settle down and have a look at how you fit into the 'system'.

THE SYSTEM AT YOUR DISPOSAL

In the next chapter I will briefly describe New Zealand's parliamentary and justice system. Here are some points about how to access it and interact with it if you need to do this.

All New Zealand citizens and residents have access to their Member of Parliament (MP). The Blue Pages at the front of your telephone directory will give contact details for the offices of electorate members, some of whom conduct 'clinics' in their electorates on Saturday mornings. If you have some concerns, you may attend one to be heard. If you write to a local MP or a cabinet minister, you will not need to affix stamps on the letter. The idea is that every Kiwi should be able to contact his or her MP, regardless of whether they can afford the 40-cent stamp for a Standard Post letter or not. Contact details for all members of the parliament and cabinet ministers are available on the website for the New Zealand Parliament found in the *Resource Guide*. If you would like to hear the debates in parliament, they have been broadcast since 1936 whenever the house convenes, and they are still on the radio today.

If your problem is with the local government, again the Blue Pages of the telephone directory will guide you. You can speak to your local city or county councillor if you are not happy with the local water quality or if you think that it is your street's turn to have the footpaths resealed. Again, there is a comparatively easy way to get heard. Unfortunately, having been heard is sometimes where the matter ends.

You may not need to see your MP or city councillor (while I know some as personal friends and acquaintances, I have never visited one in an 'official' capacity), but you may well have to see a Justice of the Peace (JP) from time to time. JPs can witness documents, take sworn statements and verify copies of your qualifications. While the government officials are listed in the Blue Pages of your telephone directory, the JPs are listed in the Yellow Pages. Just pick the one nearest your home. Their services are free, but it is a courtesy to ring in advance and make an appointment.

You may feel that you have not been treated fairly by either the central or the local government or any of its agencies or organisations, such as school boards, trustees or universities. If you have tried to settle the matter with the person or body against which you have a grievance but have not been successful, you may have the option of lodging a complaint with the Ombudsman. New Zealand introduced the Office of the Ombudsmen, which originated in Sweden, in 1962. It was the first English-speaking country to do so.

The Ombudsman is an independent arbiter of disputes between individuals and the government. If you feel that a government decision has been unlawful, unreasonable, unjust, or improperly discriminatory, you may lodge a complaint and have it investigated or, as is often the case, settled informally. The Ombudsman will also investigate if you are denied access to official information by government agencies; in every case however, it is important that you first try all the other avenues open to you before approaching the Ombudsman's office. There are now also specialist Ombudsmen for banking, insurance and savings, but they deal with complaints about private sector agencies and are not accountable to the parliamentary Ombudsmen.

One person I hope you will never have to see from the dock is a judge. If you have the misfortune to be charged with an offence and are required to attend a court, you will be notified of the date and time when you have to be there. It you do not attend the hearing, you can be arrested. You may however, ask the court for another date if there is a good reason why you cannot attend on the specified date and time. Ring the court office as early as possible to find out how to change the date. If you have to go to court as a witness, the police will let you know what you have to do.

If you are facing a charge, you can be represented free-of-charge by a duty solicitor. Again, you can arrange for this by ringing or calling at the court office in advance, but you can ask any of the court staff where to find the duty solicitor on the day you arrive for the hearing. You can, of course, also engage a private lawyer who, for a fee, will conduct your defence and advise you. The larger courts will have a desk in the public waiting area where volunteers called 'Friends of the Court' are to be found. They are specially trained to assist you.

If you do not speak and understand English, it is a good idea to bring someone with you who can help you. However, for the actual court case, an official interpreter will be required. If you let the court know that you need an interpreter, the case will be adjourned to allow one to be present. Court proceedings are held in public, and you can bring people along to support you.

If you are accused of a serious charge, you may be eligible for legal aid. This is a system of financial assistance towards the cost of a lawyer to represent you. You will be asked to make an application and will be told if it is approved. The Legal Services Agency website, listed in the *Resource Guide*, gives useful information on the process of getting legal aid.

Under New Zealand law, if you are the victim of a crime—and this can be very stressful—you do have the right to tell the court how this affected you and what assistance you may need as a result. Victim advisors, who are specially-trained people, are available to help you cope with the difficulties of a court appearance and to inform the judge of what you have suffered. Ask about this service.

Like any bureaucracy, the New Zealand government and justice systems are large and unwieldy. However, my limited experience of them has convinced me that they have checks and balances in place to ensure that no matter what position you are in, you have the right to be treated fairly and humanely, and that, as far as possible, justice is done and seen to be done. If people have complaints and grievances, there are agencies in place to ensure that they can be heard and their problems properly dealt with. I hope that you, like me so far, will never be in a position where you have to use them.

Chapter Five

KIWI BUSINESS

THE BIG PICTURE

Because of its history as a British colony, New Zealand is a constitutional monarchy under the Westminster system. Although it is just about as far away from London as you can get, the British Queen, Elizabeth II, is also queen of New Zealand. She is represented in New Zealand by the Governor-general, and like the queen, her representative remains outside the cut and thrust of politics.

While New Zealand is still a constitutional monarchy, I am not sure how much longer that will continue. The present prime minister, Helen Clark, has made it quite clear that in her view, New Zealand will become a republic in the future. In voicing this view, she is really only expressing the view of an increasing number of Kiwis. A good indicator is public reaction to royal visits that take place from time to time. The earlier visits of Queen Elizabeth II and the Duke of Edinburgh used to bring the country to a halt. People lined the route of the royal progress with flags; thousands turned up to various events where the queen would be present. Her every move and her every speech became front-page headline material in the New Zealand papers. In contrast to this, the most recent visit in 2002 was low-key. People knew the queen was in the country, but the visit no longer stirred up mass enthusiasm. The crowds were friendly but much smaller, and the headlines were more restrained. There still are many sincere and enthusiastic royalists, but their number is dwindling, and it is possible that the time when New Zealand will cut its ties with the British monarchy may not be too far away.

New Zealand is governed by its parliament, the House of Representatives. Members of parliament are elected by eligible voters (all citizens and permanent residents over the age of 18) for a three-year term. Parliament makes legislative decisions and supervises its administration and allocates funds to run New Zealand ministries, government departments and other agencies. These are known as the 'Public Sector'. All members of the parliament are elected by the 'mixed member proportional system' (MMP). This system is also used in Germany and gives each voter two votes; one for the member of parliament and one for the party. The main decision-making body in the parliament is the cabinet, presided over by the prime minister.

Many New Zealanders enjoy discussing local politics and can get quite impassioned about it. If you read the local papers, you will soon become familiar with the issues that are of burning concern to New Zealanders. If you are a newcomer, it may be wise to spend some time as a listener and spectator before expounding your own views, particularly if they concern local issues.

The judicial system is independent of the government. There are three types of court in New Zealand. The lowest, in terms of its jurisdiction, is the District Court which includes the Family Courts (for family and marriage disputes), the Youth Court, and the Disputes

Tribunal. The District Court deals with civil cases up to NZ$200,000 and criminal cases. It also regulates business activities.

The High Court deals with serious criminal cases, major civil cases and some appeals from the District Court. Finally, there is the Court of Appeal that deals with appeals from the High Court and cases after jury trials in the District Court. Up till 2004, the final appeal could be made to the Judicial Committee of the Privy Council in London. The newly formed Supreme Court of New Zealand, which replaces the Judicial Committee of the Privy Council in London, will commence hearings in July 2004.

And this is the big picture, the environment in which business and society operate in New Zealand.

Hamilton District Court.

THE BUSINESS SCENE

Over the last 20 years, the business environment in New Zealand has changed dramatically. In the 1980s, business was conducted in a highly-regulated economy, with producer subsidies and tariff protection for inefficient industries. Many key service industries, such as the railways, electricity generation and distribution, and the post office, were owned and operated by the government. Successive governments have abolished subsidies, eliminated tariffs, privatised a whole range of service industries, and dismantled a large part of the regulatory framework. The jury is still out on whether the mantra 'public ownership bad—private ownership good' has been carried too far. New Zealand's national airline, Air New Zealand, was privatised and then had to be reacquired by the government to save it from going bankrupt. To be fair, Air New Zealand enjoys the reputation of being an international airline of a high standard and it was not the only such carrier to be affected by international factors.

It is true however, that as a result of the reforms over the last two decades, the 2002 Economic Freedom of the World annual report has New Zealand in fifth place behind Hong Kong, Singapore, the United States, and the United Kingdom. What this means is that New Zealand is one of the least-regulated economies in the Asia Pacific region, with very few restrictions on businesses establishing themselves in the country. Market forces, rather than regulations, govern the type, size and location of a business. If the business is foreign-owned or the New Zealand subsidiary of a foreign company, there are tax agreements between New Zealand and 26 countries to ensure a fair tax regime. There are no restrictions on the amount of funds that may be brought into New Zealand or taken out.

There are, of course, some consents that are required if foreign investors want to set up shop in New Zealand. They would have to apply to the Overseas Investment Commission if, for example, they want to engage in commercial fishing inside New Zealand's exclusive economic zone, or if they want to purchase more than five hectares of land. This required application also extends to investments that exceed NZ$50 million. Overall, however, the New Zealand business scene is largely deregulated and operating within an open economy. Because of its size, both in terms of population and in terms of its Gross Domestic Product (GDP), New Zealand will continue to be subject to fluctuations in the global markets. Nevertheless, government policies to control inflation, reduce public debt and control public spending have produced a stable and favourable climate for business. Furthermore, New Zealand has one of the lowest average tariff rates in the world, a skilled labour force, a well-developed infrastructure and almost no corruption. The annual Corruption Perceptions Index, issued by Transparency International, consistently lists New Zealand within the top two or three countries in the world, together with Finland, Denmark, Iceland and Singapore.

One of the features of New Zealand business is that it tends to focus on niche areas where the Kiwi's natural ingenuity and inventiveness can be brought to bear. We do not have the economic or population base for large-scale business, which is why we do have branches or New Zealand partner institutions with a large number of global corporates, but the head offices are always offshore. For example, all but two of the 18 banks operating in the country are owned offshore. The New Zealand stock exchange lists more than 200 entities with a combined capitalisation of about NZ$45 billion.

The fact that most New Zealand businesses are small to medium scale does, of course, also have an upside. It provides for flexibility in meeting changing market needs and gives us the ability to keep the cost of short run, high-technology manufacturing to about a third of what they are in the United States, for example. Areas of strength and developing strength in New Zealand manufacturing are in electrical and electronic engineering, earthquake engineering, film production, wood processing (35% of the world's *pinus radiata* plantations are in New Zealand), biotechnology, call centres (our unique time-zone gives us access to the whole world for the processing of calls and data at convenient local times), tourism, and food and horticulture.

Our major strength, however, is our people and their Number-8-wire mentality that I have described in an earlier chapter. Did you know that New Zealanders developed disposable syringes, stamp vending machines, childproof medicine bottles, the electric fence, luggage carousels, and the jet boat?

CALL ME BILL

I still remember my first visit to my bank manager. True, that is now some years ago, but the basic attitudes have not changed. I dressed up for the occasion; I wore a jacket and tie and made sure that my shoes were shined and my hair combed. I fronted up to the bank ten minutes ahead of time, and the receptionist asked me to wait, a sure-fire way to increase my already considerable anxiety (after all, I was going to ask him for a loan!) At the appointed time, the receptionist, a kindly middle-aged lady, conducted me into the inner sanctum. Mr. Ward, the manager, came around from behind his desk; we shook hands and sat down. Of course I called him Mr Ward; not only was he older than me, but I was also the petitioner, as it were. (At least that is what I thought. Looking back now I realise that they were quite keen to give me a loan. I was a fairly good risk, and that first loan was the beginning of a very long customer relationship with the bank!) After I had explained my request and he had asked the relevant question about my financial situation, I must at some stage have used the words 'Mr Ward' when addressing him, because he interrupted me and said, "Don't worry about the 'Mr' stuff, just call me Bill."

I got the loan (and several loans since!), but the interview provides a model for having business meetings in New Zealand. It is always expected that you turn up on time. People will understand if you are late because of traffic problems, but these are comparatively rare and punctuality is appreciated. Business attire tends towards the conservative: suits and ties for men, suits, formal dresses, or skirts or trousers paired with a blouse and jacket for women. On an initial meeting, New Zealand businesspeople will generally be very warm and friendly, but there is a certain formality. You will use titles, exchange business cards, and shake hands (firmly, and looking at the other person, as for the social occasions already mentioned). In New Zealand, as in most Western societies, the title is used with the second (family) name, so that Mr Christopher Hinton would be addressed as 'Mr Hinton', and not 'Mr Christopher'. Women are addressed with either Mrs if married, or Miss if unmarried, although the title Ms (pronounced Miz), which does not indicate marital status, is preferred by many younger ones. Have a look at the business card, and if that is no help because it simply says 'Christine Hinton', without a title, it is perfectly in order to ask.

Once the talks get underway, your New Zealand counterpart will relax fairly quickly and may well go to first name terms sooner than in the more formal European setting. My suggestion would be to take your cue from your New Zealand conversation partner. By doing this, you will not appear to 'force' the pace or conversely to be too aloof and formal. During the conversation, New Zealanders maintain eye contact without staring at each other. If you avoid looking at your conversation partners, they may wonder whether you are trustworthy. However, if your conversation partner is Polynesian, do not be surprised if they avert their eyes when talking to you. In their culture, this is a mark of respect.

You will find that New Zealanders will be fairly direct when conducting a business conversation. They will get to the point quickly and not spend too much time on polite social conversation. This is not because they are rude, it is because business is business, and they reserve the social interaction for the informal gatherings.

In some countries, it is customary for partners in business discussions to exchange presents. This is not common in New Zealand, although business people with experience in markets where it is done, may give you a small present if you are from one of these countries. They will not expect a present in return, but will appreciate one if you have one. A small souvenir from your home country is fine. The important thing is to make sure that the present is not too large and expensive. This could be interpreted as an attempt to positively influence the outcome of the discussions and, in New Zealand, this may well have the opposite effect.

Occasionally, your New Zealand business partner will invite you to lunch to discuss business. Meals, however, are generally regarded as social occasions rather than working sessions. Certainly at dinner, small talk and general conversation is the rule, rather than negotiation and business. Incidentally, one of the worst conversational sins that you can commit when talking to a New Zealander, whether it be a business partner or a social contact, is to treat New Zealand as if it were part of Australia or to make comparisons between New Zealand and Australia to the detriment of New Zealand. If you are asked out to a social occasion, don't forget my earlier advice about giving your partner plenty of personal space.

There are a few other pitfalls that should be avoided when making polite conversation. Never ask a woman her age or weight, and never ask your conversation partner how much money they earn, or what their house or items in their house cost. Such questions are embarrassing for New Zealanders. Money and personal finances generally are not subjects for conversation with New Zealanders. I remember how much I had become a Kiwi when I returned to Switzerland some years back and attended a class reunion. Within ten minutes of talking to former classmates, they were telling me how much they earned and what (very exclusive) cars they were driving and wanted to know the same about me. I remember feeling very uncomfortable, not because I had anything to hide, but because among Kiwis, you simply don't talk about these things unless you are very good friends.

Incidentally, when you are making appointments for business meetings, most businesses are open Monday to Friday, 8:30 a.m. to 5:00 p.m. while banks are generally open from 9:00 a.m. to 4:30 p.m. In major cities, banks now also open on Saturdays and Sundays from 10:00 a.m. to 4:00 p.m. Retail stores open on Saturdays and in most larger centres and tourist resorts, on Sundays as well.

THE NERDS ARE YOUR FRIENDS

For a country that is a long way from anywhere with a small population and a high reliance on farm and primary production, New Zealand is remarkably technology-friendly and sophisticated in the use of technology. A whole number of international companies, such as Ericsson, Vodafone, BMW and IBM use New Zealand as a test bed for new inventions and technologies before they become available globally. At my university, there was a computer on the desk of every staff member at a time when in much wealthier countries, computers in universities were still locked up in special 'computer rooms', and you had to get a key from the secretary to be able to use one.

If you look at investment in information technology as a proportion of GDP, you will find that New Zealand has one of the highest percentages in the world. It is not surprising therefore to find that on a per capita basis New Zealand has one of the highest interconnect rates in the world, with over 51 access lines and 30 mobile phones per 100 persons. Wellington, in particular, has been described as the most wired city in the world.

The New Zealand government has taken the lead in the technological revolution by introducing the 'e-government programme'. Under this, it is moving to make government departments and their agencies available on the Internet 24 hours a day, seven days a week, 365 days a year. Most departments already have websites that provide information as well as application forms for various processes online. Many such websites are listed in the *Resource Guide* at the end of this book. The government itself has such a website, and the e-government portal is designed to help people find the right web page for their needs. It is already possible to register a company on the web (http://www.companies.govt.nz), and the project will eventually make it possible for New Zealanders to register a birth or death, renew their drivers licence or transact other kinds of business with the government online.

This willingness to adopt technologies is reflected both in everyday life and in the way we conduct business. My 90-year-old mother, for example, is perfectly happy to pay in the supermarket by swiping her EFTPOS (Electronic Fund Transfer at Point of Sale) card and entering her personal identification number (PIN). New Zealand was the first country in the world to have EFTPOS because, like so many new technologies, it was trialed here. It means that instead of paying cash at the supermarket, the service station or just about anywhere, (including the doctor's), you hand over your bank card and then type your four-digit PIN into a keypad. If there is enough money in your bank account, the money you owe is transferred from your account to the shop's. In supermarkets, they will even offer to give you some cash if you need it, which saves you having to go to the ATM (Automatic Teller Machine) or the bank. It is a nice turnaround of shopping customs. In the old days, you had to bring cash to the store to buy your groceries. Now, the checkout operator will ask you, 'do you want any cash with this?' EFTPOS has certainly revolutionised shopping in New Zealand. I use very little cash and now write, perhaps, no more than half a dozen cheques per year; everything else is done with plastic cards. If you do need cash, there are plenty of ATM machines: in shopping malls, at petrol stations, and outside bank branches. If there isn't one for the bank of which you are a customer, it does not matter. You can use any ATM machine, although in some cases there is a small fee if you don't use your own bank's ATM.

RED TAPE CAN BE FUN

Earlier in this chapter, I made the point that New Zealand has been found to be the fifth freest economy in the world to do business, and that certainly is true as far as regulations and controls on establishing and running businesses in New Zealand are concerned. Perhaps the most prominent act of parliament governing business competition is the Commerce Act (1986). Administered and enforced by the Commerce Commission, the act regulates business acquisitions to ensure competition in the marketplace. Like all major New Zealand government ministries, departments and agencies, the Commerce Commission has an informative website. The listing can be found in the *Resource Guide*.

If you want to start a business in New Zealand, there are not many legal hurdles to overcome, as we have seen. One of the things you may want to consider however, is the name under which you are going to trade. If your first language is not English, it would be helpful if you check with an English-speaking friend whether the name you have chosen is suitable. I recently saw a sign in a New Zealand town advertising the 'Know-all Group Ltd'. A 'know-all' in New Zealand is a person who thinks that they always know everything better, in other words an unpleasant person who will always try to correct you.

If the business was trying to attract Kiwi customers, the name would certainly put people off.

While the regulatory environment for business in New Zealand is free and helpful, there is a strong framework of legislation that protects the environment, the workers, and the consumers. Now don't get me wrong! I am not a lawyer, and what I am giving you here is not legal advice, but simply a brief description of some of the legislation that applies to business in New Zealand.

Environment Protection

The principal piece of legislation that protects the environment is the Resource Management Act (1991). This act gives local and regional government the responsibility of promoting "sustainable management of physical and natural resources". This includes land-use management, noise control, water, soil and geothermal resource management, pollution control, protection against natural hazards, soil conservation and other aspects pertaining to land use. The purpose of the act is to maintain New Zealand's clean and green environment so that it continues to be a reality and not just an image.

Workplace Protection

Workers' rights are safeguarded in the Employment Relations Act (2000). It governs collective employment contracts negotiated between employers and unions, although individual contracts are also provided for. One of the underlying principles is that parties to an employment relationship must deal with each other in good faith, which means that they must deal honestly and openly with each other. Unions have 'reasonable' access to the workplace under the Act, and a mediation service to deal with disputes is put in place.

Other legislation to regulate workplace relationships include the Minimum Wages Act (1991), that provides for a minimum wage for workers over the age of 18, the Holidays Act (2003) that gives

workers a minimum of three weeks' paid annual leave (to be increased to four weeks with effect from 1 April 2007) after 12 months of employment. Workers are also entitled to the 11 days of statutory holidays. Safety in the workplace is regulated by the Health and Safety in Employment Act (1992). The Parental Leave and Employment Protection Act (2002) allows primary caregivers up to 12 weeks' paid leave. To receive this, you must have worked for the same employer for at least 10 hours per week for a whole year before the birth of the child. The various dollar figures to be paid out for maternity leave is subject to periodic revision and variation. More information about workers protection can be found on the websites of the Employment Relations Service and the Human Resources Institute of New Zealand. The websites are listed in the *Resource Guide*.

Finally, New Zealand law, namely the Human Rights Act (1993), prohibits discrimination against an employee or job applicant on the basis of sex, marital status, religion, colour, race, ethnicity, national origin, disability, age, political views, employment status, family status, sexual orientation or union involvement.

The Human Rights Act obviously has implications for you if you would like to appoint staff. Some years back, I chaired an appointments panel that was going to appoint a lecturer in an Asian language. Since nobody on the panel spoke the language, I invited a Christian minister of religion from that particular country to participate in the appointments process which included, of course, an interview with the shortlisted candidates. At some point in the interview, the minister conducted the interview in the language the applicants were going to teach in order to establish that they had adequate knowledge of it. A week after the interviews, we received a complaint from one of the candidates. It appears that the minister had asked several questions about their religious beliefs. These clearly were not relevant to the position the candidate had applied for, and I had to apologize for what were not just inappropriate but actually illegal questions under New Zealand legislation.

When interviewing candidates for a job in your firm, you will therefore have to be careful not to ask questions that could indicate an intention to discriminate on any of the prohibited categories in the Human Rights Act. For example, it is fine to ask somebody whether they would be available to work on Saturdays, but it is not acceptable to ask them whether they are Jewish or Muslim.

Consumer Protection

Consumers are looked after principally by two acts. The first is the Fair Trading Act (1986), which deals with misleading or deceptive advertising or claims, false representations, unfair practices, consumer information and the safety of products or services. The second, the Consumer Guarantees Act (1993), sets up a series of warranties that apply to any product. Under this act, the consumer has a right to compensation if an article or service contains defects or is unfit for the purpose for which it was purchased.

While these acts are there for the protection of workers and the public, they are invoked comparatively rarely by people like me. My daughter recently saw a poster advertisement in a shop window for a dinner set that was reduced quite considerably 'while stocks last'. When she tried to purchase the set, the salesperson told her that the 'special' had expired at the end of the month and that if she wanted the set (yes, it was on the shelf and she was standing in front of it), she would have to pay the full price. My daughter only had to politely murmur 'Fair Trading Act!', and the salesperson went to the telephone to talk to the manager of the shop, who agreed that she could have the set at the reduced price. When she went to pick it up, the poster had been removed from the shop window!

Income Tax

While we are on rules and regulations, I might as well deal with a subject that is not universally liked, but of universal interest: tax.

Company tax for resident and non resident companies is 33%. Personal tax is levied at source (i.e. you employer deducts it from your pay cheque before you get the loot) and is 19.5% for the income bracket of NZ$0–$38,000, 33% for income between $38,001 and $60,000, while any income above $60,001 is taxed at 39%. This system of taxing income at the source is called PAYE (pay-as-you-earn) in New Zealand, and it is administered by the Inland Revenue Department (IRD). As soon as you begin to earn income in New Zealand (even if it is only interest on a bank account), you will need an IRD number. The IRD website, listed in the *Resource Guide*, will give you details of how to go about getting one.

In addition to income tax, New Zealand has a Goods and Services Tax of 12.5% that is levied on just about anything and that I have already talked about when discussing shopping in the last chapter.

The only major exemptions from GST are financial services, services performed as an employee, and residential rental accommodation.

In New Zealand these are the taxes you will pay as an individual (and the rates are, of course, changed from time to time by successive governments). There is no capital gains tax, no estate duties, and apart from local government rates (dues for water, refuse collection, and civic amenities that are levied as a percentage of the assessed value of your property), there are no local taxes.

And with this, you have the bad news. The good news is what the New Zealand government is doing with these taxes, and this will be the subject of the next chapter.

Chapter Six

FROM THE CRADLE TO THE GRAVE

MEDICAL CARE

This is a very embarrassing story, but I have to tell it to illustrate a point about the New Zealand health system. It happened some years ago, and I was quite a bit younger (and perhaps more foolish) at the time. As I was walking across the university campus, I was struck by the sight of a very attractive female. It appears that I was so struck that I was not watching where I was going and, as a result, my right foot struck a very low concrete nib wall with a real crunch. Chastened, I hobbled to my car, and as my big toe started to swell up, I decided to go to the doctor and have it checked out. As I fronted up to the desk, the receptionist asked me whether my appointment was 'accident related', as indeed it was. The doctor examined my toe (I did not tell him the reason for the accident!) and then sent me off to have it x-rayed. One of the bones in my toe did indeed have a crack in it but fortunately, it healed well.

The important part of the story is not the reason for my fractured toe, but the fact that it was an accident. In New Zealand, that means that my doctor, who usually happily charges me around NZ$45 for a consultation, did not charge me a single cent. My x-ray was also free. The reason was that my foolish accident, like any accident that causes injury in New Zealand, was covered by the government-run Accident Rehabilitation and Compensation Insurance scheme (ACC). Under this scheme, anyone that suffers an accident is covered, regardless of whether they are New Zealand citizens or not and whether the accident was their fault or not. However, the ACC will decide how an accident is defined for the purposes of your claim for compensation and whether your injury fits within their definition. They may disagree with your understanding, in which case you have the right of appeal. If you are a tourist in New Zealand and have the misfortune of having a car accident, your medical costs will be met. Unfortunately, this does not apply to damage to the vehicles. As I said in an earlier chapter, it is very important that you have car insurance. You will also need medical insurance to cover treatment if you fall ill, since ordinary illnesses are not covered by ACC.

If you have the misfortune to be involved in an accident, ACC can help you in many ways. It will help with the cost of medical or dental treatment, hospital treatment or surgery, prescription or x-rays, and the transport to have treatment and related accommodation costs. It will even compensate you for lost earnings, but only if you have been earning regular wages in New Zealand. This means that if you are a tourist and have a regular job outside New Zealand, you will not qualify for this benefit. For people living and working in this country, ACC will provide rehabilitation services, home support, aids and appliances such as wheelchairs, and even modifications to the home where this is necessary. If the injury results in death, there are death benefits, such as subsidies for funeral costs and survivor benefits.

All in all, ACC does give a pretty comprehensive cover, and the scheme is simple because it applies to everybody. Occasionally, you

find some letter writers to the daily papers that get very excited when they hear in the news that a burglar received an ACC payout for an injury he sustained while carrying out a burglary. The other side of the coin is that, while your are covered 24 hours a day, you cannot yourself bring an action for compensation for injury against the person or firm whose fault may have caused your accident.

If you fall ill in New Zealand, you will have access to a world-class health system. It is financed mainly by the state, through taxes, although over the last couple of decades, private providers have increased substantially, as has the purchasing of private health insurance. As I have said earlier, you will still have to pay for the privilege of accessing the New Zealand health system unless you are a New Zealand citizen or have a Residence Permit. New Zealanders pay something between NZ$35 and NZ$45 for a visit to their doctor, less for children, and nothing at all for children under six years of age. Hospitals and maternity care are free for New Zealand citizens and permanent residents. You can choose to have a private provider

149

which, in the case of hospitals, may mean that you don't have to go on a waiting list, particularly if the surgery is not urgent. As a rule, private hospitals only provide selective health care; all acute conditions are dealt with by public hospitals. If you have to be transported by ambulance or air as a patient to a public hospital, you will be expected to contribute to the cost of the service.

Maternity Care

Maternity and childcare services are mainly provided free-of-charge to those who are eligible. Most births take place in hospitals with a discharge home after 48 hours if all is well. For six weeks after a baby is born, a midwife is available to make home visits and to ensure mother and baby are progressing normally. New Zealand has a unique service provided for babies and young children by specialised nurses called Plunket nurses. They are situated in the community and run clinics and make home visits. Their role is to ensure that the child progresses normally and to detect any problems which can then be referred for treatment if necessary.

Dental Care

Dental care for adults is not cheap. There is however, free dental care for children up to the age of 16, or 18 if they are still in school. Non-essential procedures (for example, orthodontics) on children are not covered by the free service and will therefore incur a cost.

Doctors

Primary healthcare is provided by the general practitioner (GP), who will refer you to a specialist if required. You might be referred to a private or public specialist. If you choose a private specialist, you have to pay substantially more but can choose your specialist and will not have to wait too long for a consultation. If you go to a public specialist, your health status must first be assessed on a scoring system that determines how soon you should be seen, and your case will be classified as urgent, semi-urgent, or non-urgent. For non-urgent cases, there can sometimes be quite a considerable wait. You can telephone the hospital to find out where you are on the waiting list. Sometimes, if you are available at short notice, you may get in earlier if there is a last minute cancellation. Your chances of getting treatment are greatly improved if you keep the hospital or clinic informed of any changes to your address or telephone number. Do let the hospital know before your appointment if for some reason you are unable to attend. This is very important because a missed appointment, without due notification, may not be rescheduled.

If you have an existing condition and have a copy of your medical records, x-rays or scans, it will be helpful to bring them to the doctor who will be treating you.

There is no shortage of doctors in New Zealand, at least, not overall. In 2002, there were 8403 active doctors, whereas in 1983, there were 5403. There are, of course, shortages in fields where there is generally a global shortage, such as for psychiatrists. There are also often shortages in rural areas, since most doctors prefer to work in a city where they have easy access to major hospitals.

Group Practices

Nowadays, most doctors work in group practices, which means that they can share administrative and other facilities. Most New Zealanders have a regular doctor whom they visit at the group practice when they have need of their services. Attached to these practices are usually a laboratory (for the collection of samples and specimens), a radiology department for x-rays and scans, and a chemist for dispensing medication. A physiotherapist service is often attached to the group practice.

Emergency Centres and Hospitals

Another development that has occurred over the last couple of decades is the emergence, particularly in the larger cities, of privately run 24-hour emergency centres. You pay a higher fee but can get access to a doctor without having to make an appointment. The drawback is that you do not get to develop a relationship with 'your' GP because you may not see the same doctor on consecutive visits. I have however, found the local centre very handy when I needed some medical attention in the weekend or in the evening when the medical centre that I normally visit was closed. Some of these facilities are actually staffed by a collective of the local GPs and you may just be lucky enough to encounter your own GP there.

Large public hospitals have an Accident and Emergency (A&E) department. These are reserved for acute medical cases and serious accidents. If a person is experiencing chest pain, shortness of breath, heavy bleeding or a seizure (fit), it is best to ring the ambulance service on 111 or take them at once to the public hospital rather than to the private emergency centre. People are encouraged to use the private centres for less serious health problems.

A Note on Communication

Larger practices and hospitals will have interpreters available to assist with translation. If the patient does not speak English or does not speak and understand it well, it is a good idea to take along a family member who can speak English. Many of the forms and instruction booklets are available in a range of languages, so please ask if a suitable one is available for your use or your family's if they need it. If you prefer to have a female doctor, your chances are improving. In 2001, 32.6% of New Zealand doctors were female, up from 16.6% twenty years earlier.

Slap On That Sunscreen

There are few health risks when living in New Zealand, but there is one in particular that my Malaysian nephew knows all too well. One day, while I was out sailing with him in the Hauraki Gulf, I strongly advised him to rub some sunblock. "Oh, I don't need that, Uncle", he said, "I have a built-in suntan!" as he pointed to his brown skin. He got very little sleep that night with his sunburned face, arms and back.

Because of the thin ozone layer and the absence of air pollution, it is very easy to get severe sunburn in New Zealand, and you are strongly advised to cover up and protect your skin while outdoors. New Zealand has one of the highest rates of skin cancer in the world. A lot of it can be prevented if you make sure that you take precautions: put on some sunscreen regularly when you are outdoors and wear a sunhat and sunglasses.

You don't have to overdo it though. A few years ago, there was quite a lot of publicity about the size of the hole in the ozone layer over the South Pole. At a conference in Auckland, I met a whole lot of colleagues from Europe who had arrived here afraid that they would get zapped by the sun. They were very surprised to find that we did not live in underground bunkers, between which we would scurry when necessary to avoid undue exposure to the sun. One of the great features of New Zealand life is that you can spend so much of it outdoors. All you need are a few sensible precautions and you will find that your health will actually benefit from being out in the sun and fresh air.

When you are in a foreign country, it is always good to know that you have access to competent medical help when you need it. You can be assured that you have that while you are in New Zealand.

EDUCATION

I have never forgotten the culture shock I received on my first day in a New Zealand school. For starters, I had to dress up in short trousers, a nondescript grey shirt, no tie, and a funny little hat (which has, thank goodness, been abandoned by most New Zealand schools, although schoolchildren are encouraged to wear sunhats in the playground). During the two years before my parents immigrated to New Zealand, I had gone to school dressed in long trousers, a jacket and collar and tie. I therefore felt a bit conspicuous standing at the roadside waiting for the school bus to take me to town where I had been enrolled in one of the high schools.

Things did not improve on the way into town. As we approached town, the bus started to fill up and finally there were no seats left. A girl got on at the next stop and, as I had always done on the train in Switzerland, I stood up and offered her my seat. Big mistake! The bus exploded in ribald laughter and comments that, probably fortunately, I could not fully understand since my English was still basic. The girl blushed, covered in confusion and embarrassment. I sheepishly sat down again. Lesson Number One: it was not 'cool' for adolescents to show adult manners.

I did not take long to adapt however, and I thoroughly enjoyed my time at school, and after that, at the university. My experience of primary school rests on having our three children go through the system, and my overall impression of those years is that the emphasis in New Zealand schools is on informality and cooperative teaching and learning, rather than on a strictly enforced hierarchical system that I have observed in other cultures.

There are three types of schools in New Zealand. The majority are state schools, and most of such schools are co-educational, that is, boys and girls attend the same school. There are some single-sex schools, particularly in the larger cities. The school I went to in Hamilton was a state boys' school, and it did feel strange to me because I had had all my previous education in co-educational schools in Switzerland. State schools are funded by the government, and attendance is free for New Zealanders and permanent residents. A small donation or 'activity fee' is usually charged. The second type of school is the private school, where fees are charged for attendance. Private schools are often owned and operated by churches, and they must meet government standards. In some centres, there are also private schools that subscribe to a particular philosophy of education, such as Montessori and Rudolph Steiner schools. The third type is the integrated school. These are former private schools that are now government-funded and teach the state curriculum. They maintain their particular philosophy and may teach it. They also charge fees, but because they receive government funds, these fees are lower than those charged by the private schools.

The school year in New Zealand runs from February to December. It is divided into four terms by three holidays of two to three weeks. The long break is, of course, between December and February, when the weather is hottest in New Zealand.

Schooling is compulsory for children from the ages of six to 16, but for most, formal schooling starts when they are somewhere between three and five years old. It is the period which is called 'Early Childhood Education' here, and a whole range of preschool institutions and facilities cater to this age group. Playcentres, kindergartens, playgroups and home-based services are available, but unique to New Zealand are the Maori language nests, *kohanga reo*, where all teaching is done in Maori. There are also some Pacific Island language schools also designed to foster the use of the child's first language.

An elementary school in a suburb.

The Early Years and Onwards

Early childhood education in New Zealand is characterised by its informal approach. Learning takes place by playing rather than by formal instruction. You may also find that some preschool institutions will not take your child for five days a week. The New Zealand approach to schooling, particularly at pre-school level, has caused some parents, particularly from Asian countries, some difficulties. They find it difficult to understand that their child is learning even though he or she is not sitting at a desk arranged in a straight row in front of a teacher that stays at the front of the room and lectures to the children. It is indeed a different approach and it leaves the children much more freedom than the formal approach.

Some time ago, I was the guest of a Chinese provincial government, together with several hundred guests from all over the world who had come to a particular conference. The formal welcome involved hundreds of small school children who were standing in long rows, singing and waving flowers at various stages of the proceedings. It was a very hot day and the welcome was outdoors. I remember being absolutely amazed at the discipline of the children. They stood there, totally still when required, did their thing whenever it was their turn, and then stood at attention again during the whole hour-long ceremony. I remarked to the person standing next to me that you would never get New Zealand children to do this. This kind of discipline would be quite foreign to them. I would like to reassure parents from more formal societies that the New Zealand approach does not produce little monsters that are totally out of control, neither does it produce children who have not been schooled as well as elsewhere, quite the contrary, as we shall see a little bit further on.

Subject to some flexibility, most New Zealand children start primary school on their fifth birthday, unlike children in many other countries, where they all start at the same time once they have reached school age. The individual child is placed into a 'new entrants' room and then moves up the ladder over six years when, at the age of 10, he or she transfers to an intermediate school where these are available. If not, some primary schools go right up to year 8 or age 12. Some primary schools provide after-school care for children whose parents cannot be home when school finishes at 3:00 p.m.

After two years at intermediate school, the child then enters secondary school, also known as 'high school', 'college' or 'area school'. At this stage, all students must take compulsory 'core' subjects: English, social studies, mathematics, science and physical education. These are supplemented by electives that vary from school to school. Several sets of coherent 'electives' are often offered. From year 11 onwards, students begin to specialise in the subjects they will offer for the National Certificate of Educational Achievement (NCEA), a new New Zealand qualifications framework that is being introduced into the country between 2002 and 2004. High school finishes with year 13, when the student typically is 17 years of age.

There are five groups of tertiary level institutions in New Zealand: the eight universities; 21 polytechnics (although many of them have now adopted names, such as 'Institute of Technology'); four colleges of education (which are New Zealand's teacher training institutions); three *wananga* (Maori tertiary institutions, specializing particularly in Maori culture); and 506 private training establishments, including English language schools. All these institutions may apply to the New Zealand Qualifications Authority to offer degrees, but the range of degrees they offer are often more limited than those offered by the eight universities.

New Zealand university degrees and diplomas are accepted by major institutions all over the world as of equivalent standing. In some cases, where professional qualifications are concerned, special conditions may apply. The same holds for foreign qualifications in New Zealand, of course, so that immigrants who want to obtain registration as engineers, accountants, medical practitioners, for example, will have to find out from the appropriate registration body what requirements they have to meet.

Correspondence Schools

For children who live in very remote areas and cannot or do not wish to attend boarding school, for children or young people whose circumstances do not allow them to attend school (young mothers, prison inmates), and for students whose school is unable to provide a particular course, there is always the Correspondence School of New Zealand. With its 20,000 pupils from levels between early childhood to senior secondary levels, it is the largest school in New Zealand. From 1937 to 1990, some of the lessons were broadcast on the radio. I remember listening in at times and how I was impressed with the quality of the lessons. Nowadays, it is all done with audio cassettes and workbooks that are sent to the pupils on a weekly basis. The lessons are increasingly on the Internet. The correspondence school is also an important avenue for 'second chance' education for adults who left school without having gained a qualification and now want to remedy this.

The Quality of a New Zealand Education

By international standards, the quality of New Zealand education is very high. In the year 2000, the Organisation for Economic Co-operation and Development (OECD), under the Programme for International Student Assessment (PISA), examined 15-year old students across 40 countries (most of which were OECD member countries). New Zealand was among the six best-performing countries for reading literacy, mathematical literacy and scientific literacy. So any parents whose own cultural background makes them worried that the New Zealand approach is too informal can rest assured. It may look as if no learning is taking place, but the results show that it does take place, and the children and young people will emerge from it with achievements that put them into the top bracket of OECD countries.

The tertiary sector, particularly the universities, is also attracting an ever-increasing number of students from all over the world. This is because they can offer world-class education for a very reasonable cost, both in terms of the cost of tuition and the cost of living. The large numbers of international students have led to some problems, particularly since the attitude to study and authority is different in other parts of the world. Students from North America, Europe and Australia generally have no problems studying in New Zealand. Students from Asia, however, not only have to overcome the language barrier, they also have to learn to treat their sources differently and make sure that they scrupulously acknowledge any authority they cite. My university has now printed a special pamphlet to bring this to their attention. The other problem of which I have personal experience is that Asian students tend to regard their teachers as 'authorities' (which, hopefully they are), and find it very difficult to engage in academic debate with them. I remember how hard it was for me to teach some of my Asian students to argue with me, and how hard it was for them to do so.

When I talk to students who have arrived in New Zealand to study, I always give them two pieces of advice: Firstly, make the effort to reach out to New Zealand students. I have already referred to this in an earlier chapter when I talked about making friends. My second piece of advice is; work hard, but not too hard. Make sure you also have some fun. And this is going to be the topic of the next section.

RECREATION AND SPORT

When I made my application for New Zealand citizenship, I had to present myself for an interview with an official of what was then the Internal Affairs Department. I still remember it quite well. There were the usual questions, such as had I ever been in trouble with the law (I hadn't), did I have a bank account (I did), what were my plans for the future (I didn't quite know at that time). Then came the knockout question: had I ever been to a rugby match as a spectator. My heart fell, I considered telling a lie, but being basically an honest person, I admitted that I had never attended a rugby game. My interviewer threw up his hands in mock horror and indicated that my chances of

getting accepted as a New Zealand citizen were very slim indeed. I'm glad to say that the authorities relented and I did get accepted. I have also attended the odd rugby match since then with my sons, who were born here and have therefore been part of this Kiwi culture of sport and outdoor activity.

Rugby

Rugby has been, and still is, the glamour sport of New Zealand. Some commentators have gone so far as to declare it New Zealand's state religion. The All Blacks, the New Zealand Rugby Union team, are national heroes and some have been elevated into almost god-like positions. One of the famous All Blacks, Don Clarke, left New Zealand for South Africa in 1976 and lived there until his death in December 2002. A memorial service was held for him in New Zealand that attracted crowds of mourners.

It is true that the All Blacks are a remarkable phenomenon. Their name comes from their all-black uniform which, combined with the ferocious *haka* that they dance before every game, has struck fear into the hearts of many of their opponents. Like all sports teams, they have their ups and downs, but overall, since the beginning of international rugby over a hundred years ago, New Zealand rugby teams have been successful. When you come to New Zealand, you will find that they will inevitably be the subject of many social conversations.

Another popular topic of conversation is the Super 12 League. This is a competition between 12 Rugby League teams in South Africa, Australia and New Zealand. Five of them—based in Auckland, Hamilton, Wellington, Christchurch and Dunedin—are from New Zealand, another three are from Australia, and four are from South Africa. Again, if you want to hold your own in Monday morning conversations, you will do well to be up to date with the latest match scores and the standings of the various teams in the competition.

There are many national teams that deserve mention; when you compare the population size of New Zealand with other countries and thus take into account the limited pool of sports participants, New Zealand does remarkably well in international terms. The New Zealand cricket team is seen as a force in international cricket, and the Silver Ferns, the New Zealand netball team, is consistently within the top teams in world competition.

For somebody coming from a culture that sees sport as an admittedly desirable activity, but one that is organised (if it is organised at all) outside the school curriculum, I was surprised to learn that, like all my classmates, as part of my schooling, I was expected to participate in some kind of sport. I chose rowing and became part of a rowing team that practised regularly on the Waikato River and had a teacher as coach. I also participated in various school rowing regattas in the area. Most of my friends played rugby, hockey, soccer, netball and cricket—that delightfully crazy English game in which a full match lasts five days and nobody really knows for sure until the last overs have been bowled which team is going to win or whether it will be a draw (or worse still, the outcome can be determined several days in advance).

School competition games are usually played on Saturday mornings, so if you have school-age children, you will spend at least Saturday morning ferrying your offspring to various parks and sportsgrounds and then standing on the sideline cheering them on. Just be careful that you don't become over-exuberant in your support. There have been court cases where parents were prosecuted for hitting parents from the opposing team and the referee with umbrellas!

I had never been able to understand the rules of cricket until one Saturday morning I arrived with my cricket-playing son at the venue of a game between his school and another school team from the country. When I arrived, the organiser came up to me and told me that our side had to provide an umpire to stand out in the field and rule on various matters. I appeared to be the only parent available and when I explained that I knew absolutely nothing about cricket, my objections were ignored. I was sent out together with a parent from the opposing team who had played cricket at district level and therefore knew a lot about the game. It turned out he knew far too much. He kept on explaining the finer points of the game while I was frantically trying to learn how to fill in the score sheet.

I did learn about the game though, and by umpiring in some schoolboy games, I joined the estimated 300,000 New Zealanders who are involved in sport as organisers, managers, umpires and referees. New Zealanders love their sport, and the regular Saturday morning matches are the training ground for the players that later join the provincial teams and, if they are really top class, the national teams, such as the All Blacks or the Silver Ferns, who, in 1999, were beaten in the world championships by Australia by one single, heartbreaking goal! The New Zealanders did have their revenge though. In 2003, they defeated the Australians 49–47 and regained their world champion title. Many Kiwis have one or several Australian relatives, so the friendly rivalry often extends into families.

But as we have seen, you will find New Zealanders achieving world-class results in many other sports. Perhaps, the most famous is

Sir Edmund Hillary, the Kiwi beekeeper who, with Sherpa Tenzing Norgay, was the first to climb Mount Everest on 29 May 1953. Hillary, who is still alive, had a distinguished career as an adventurer. He established the Sir Edmund Hillary Himalayan Trust foundation that has enabled the construction of two hospitals and 27 schools in Nepal. He has also become a New Zealand icon, and his picture appears on our five-dollar note. What has endeared him to generations of New Zealanders is not only his success in climbing Mount Everest, but his laconic comment when he returned from the summit. He greeted his fellow Kiwi and expedition member George Lowe with the words, "Well, George, we've knocked the bastard off!".

Water Sports

Because of New Zealand's wonderful natural features, many other outdoor activities are available. Water sports are particularly popular, with our long coastlines and lakes; fishing is a hobby that a large proportion of the population enjoy. I myself have spent many happy hours bobbing about on the ocean with a fishing line over the stern of a small boat, and occasionally I have even caught something. As I write this, I can see the framed certificate on the wall that attests to me having hooked, fought (for an hour and a quarter!) and brought alongside the boat an 180 kg (397 pounds) Striped Marlin that we then tagged and released (I could not bear to have the beautiful fish killed). Recreational fishing at sea, incidentally, does not require a licence, but there are limits to the number and size of fish you can catch. Fishing in inland waters also has rules regarding size and number of fish that may be taken. In addition, you will have to get a licence (for a fee) for this kind of fishing.

For newcomers to New Zealand, it is particularly important to make sure that you know the rules that govern the taking of fish and shellfish. There is an abundance of excellent seafood available around New Zealand's seashores. Recently, there have been some cases of immigrants illegally taking huge quantities of shellfish. There are

Kayaking is popular during the summer.

fisheries inspectors, and if you are caught with too many fish or shellfish, or if they are undersize, you may get fined and have your boat and fishing gear confiscated. As always, it is a matter of making sure that you have the right information because ignorance of the law is no defence. The website of the Ministry of Fisheries, listed in the *Resource Guide*, has a useful summary of the rules as well as local restrictions where they exist. If you do not have access to the Internet, the Ministry can be reached by phone. Its number will be listed in the Blue Pages at the beginning of your telephone directory. Incidentally, it is a Maori custom to return the first fish caught in an outing back to the sea, as a sacrifice to *Tangaroa*, the god of the sea.

Boating

Boating is also very popular, and for some years, New Zealand held the famous America's Cup yachting trophy. The city of Auckland has the highest number of boats per capita in the world. As a result of the great interest in boats and boating, New Zealand has a thriving boat-building industry which has acquired an international reputation for excellent workmanship and, just as important, reasonable prices. I am sure that you will also want to enjoy water sports. The important thing is that you will have to adhere to a few safety rules. Unfortunately, there have been quite a number of deaths of foreigners who were not aware of these rules. One of them is that on many beaches, there can be dangerous currents. There are however, lifeguards and they usually mark the safe and patrolled parts of the beach with flags. Always swim between these flags. Your life could depend on it!

Yachts docked at an Auckland marina.

The lifeguards are only on duty in the summer months and on holidays and weekends. If there are no lifeguards on duty, ask one of the locals if it is safe to swim. There is a beach called Hot Water Beach on the Coromandel Peninsula, and the name is exactly what it is. When the tide is out, you go to the edge of the water and dig yourself a small bathtub in the sand. It will quickly fill with hot water and you have your very own (if temporary) spa. However, it is very deceptive because a rip (a strong tidal current) can develop very quickly, and several people have drowned because they stayed too long and were swept out to sea by the rip. The most dangerous time on the beaches is when the tide is turning because dangerous undercurrents can suddenly form, catching swimmers unaware.

When going out boating, it is important to keep an eye on the weather. In New Zealand, the weather can change very quickly, and what is a beautiful morning with a gentle breeze can turn into a gale in just a few hours. The Meteorological Service of New Zealand (MetService) provides regularly updated marine weather forecasts. You can get them for a nominal fee on the telephone (at the time of writing this book, the fee is NZ$1.30 per minute). The number is listed in the telephone directory under 'MetPhone'.

A few years ago, a Chinese lady bought a motor boat for her son and his family. They had never owned a boat before and lacked the experience to inspect it properly. The boat she had bought was totally unseaworthy, and on their first outing, it began to sink. Fortunately, someone saw that they were in difficulties and rang up the coastguard who sent a patrol boat to rescue them. So my second piece of advice is: take somebody with you who knows about boats when you intend to buy one, and perhaps, also take them with you on your first few trips if you are not experienced. Again, your life could depend on it! Finally, even if you are a good swimmer, always wear a lifejacket when you go out boating. Your life...(well, you know what I was going to say!) Enjoy your swimming and fishing and boating. New Zealand has beautiful water scenery, but remember to exercise caution

Tramping

Another set of leisure activities that makes use of New Zealand's wonderful resources is walking and tramping (hiking). New Zealand has thousands of walking tracks, ranging from gentle half-hour walks through a bush or meadow, to treks of several days with overnight accommodation in huts. Some of these have become very popular indeed. The Milford track, in the southwest of the South Island, has been described as the finest walk on earth. It takes four days to walk, and you spend the three nights in rather well-appointed huts. You will have to book to walk the track because usage is restricted to a small number of walkers each day. Another famous track close to the Milford track is the Routeburn track, which takes three days to walk. Like the Milford track, the scenery is beautiful.

You do not have to be superfit to walk some of the well-known tracks, and you have two options. You can either 'free walk', where you have to carry in a backpack all your clothes and food for the three to four days, or else you can take a 'guided walk'. In this case, you only

Breathtaking scenery can be expected on walking trails.

need to have a light day-pack and all your food and heavy clothing is transported for you. Your accommodation on a guided walk is reserved. For free walkers, it is by 'first-come-first-served' in separate huts.

The best information on many of the walking tracks is on the website of the New Zealand Department of Conservation (DOC) which is given in the *Resource Guide* at the back of this book. It contains descriptions of all the tracks, detailed instructions on how to get there, how to make bookings and other information you might need to embark on hiking trips. The DOC website also contains descriptions of some of the 125 walkways scattered around the country. These are easier and shorter than the major tracks, and are absolutely ideal for family use or for aspiring trampers who want to get fit to walk one of the big ones. Check out the website, or call in at one of the DOC offices. There are bound to be some walkways close to where you live.

Again, as with water sports, it is useful to observe a few precautions. While the New Zealand bush does not harbour any major danger such as wild animals, the most common danger is that you may get overtaken by bad weather or lost or both. So it is advisable to always take some extra clothing, food and water. Another important rule is to never deviate from the track. Do not take what looks like a tempting short cut. You may become lost. In the dense New Zealand bush, this can happen quite easily, so stick to the track.

A safety rule that applies both to those enjoying themselves on the sea or in the bush is that you should always tell someone in as much detail as you can, where you intend to go and when you intend to return. Don't keep your favourite fishing spot secret so that if you can't start the engine of your boat, you are stuck for the night or longer. If you get into trouble, someone will be able to ring the police and initiate a search if you are seriously overdue. New Zealand has very good rescue services. The volunteer coastguard patrols the coast and is ready and trained to help, while there are volunteer search partie for accidents in the bush. For serious cases, rescue helicopters operate from all major towns. But if you adhere to the few safety tips I have suggested, treat your environment with respect and avoid taking any unnecessary risks, you will be able to have a great time without getting into trouble.

Sport and recreation is a big part of New Zealand life, and there is even a government body—Sport and Recreation New Zealand— that was formed in February 2002 to coordinate various initiatives and schemes in this area. To meet their key aims, programmes have been developed to encourage more physical exercise among the general population, to help and train sports officials at all levels and across all sports, and to work together with other bodies to provide opportunities, to encourage people to take more exercise.

While Sports and Recreation New Zealand has only recently begun its work, indications are that New Zealanders are perhaps becoming a bit more active. A survey in 1997 found that 33% of the population was physically active for less than 2.5 hours per week. This figure is described as the 'Couch Potato Index'. The survey was repeated in 2000, and the Couch Potato Index had dropped to 30%.

One of the attractive features of sport in New Zealand is that it is, like most Kiwi institutions, comparatively egalitarian. There are few barriers to access. I remember in my teens working as a ballboy in a tennis club in Switzerland. Tennis and golf were sports that could only be played by people who could afford the comparatively high costs associated with them. In New Zealand, there are no such restrictions. Most schools have tennis courts, and if they are not used, parents may well be able to have a hit if they ask the principal nicely. Green fees at public golf courses are also within the means of the average Kiwi, and even club memberships are quite reasonable, although there are, of course, exclusive clubs. My Japanese friends are always astonished at how cheap playing golf in New Zealand is. This is not altogether surprising: New Zealand has the highest number of golf courses per capita in the world.

TOURISM

When the global travel editor of the Lonely Planet series of travel guides ran a survey among his staff to see which they considered the top five places to visit in 2003, the top destination was New Zealand. This is not altogether surprising. After the horrifying events of September 11, 2001, and after the publicity from the movie *Lord of the Rings*, New Zealand is seen as a clean, green country that is also safe to visit.

If you take away the overheated hype of advertising, it is true that New Zealand is a very desirable destination for tourists. The problem is that there is just too much to do and see for one visit, and if you are in New Zealand for a few years, you may be lucky enough to fit in several holidays. Most of my and my family's holidays have been in New Zealand, and we still haven't seen all of it.

You can go up north, to visit the historic little townships and mission stations where the first Europeans established themselves, as well as the grounds on which the Treaty of Waitangi was signed. But

in addition to all that, you also have superb coastal scenery and indigenous forests where kauri trees have grown since Christ preached the gospel in Palestine.

You can go to the Auckland region, where you have all the excitement of city entertainment, shopping and nightlife, complete with a casino and night clubs, but at the same time be surrounded by great beaches and idyllic islands. A little bit further south, you come to the Waitomo Caves, underground limestone caverns in which you are taken on a boat ride on an underground river to see the thousands and thousands of glow-worms that live there. Then there is Rotorua, the centre of Maori cultural activity and a thermal wonderland. I have already mentioned Lake Taupo, the volcanic crater the size of Singapore where you can catch trout in its crystal waters. Go west from Taupo and find yourself on the volcanic plateau with its active volcanoes; one of which is Mt. Ruapehu where you can go skiing in winter. Just be careful if you go up to the summit; the water in the crater lake, although surrounded by snow, is hot. Go further west and discover historical New Plymouth, one of the original New Zealand Company settlements, with its magnificent backdrop of Mount Taranaki, a snow-tipped cone volcano that rivals Mount Fuji in Japan. And finally, there is Wellington, the nation's capital, with its hills, each of which affords a vista of the harbour, its government offices, diplomatic posts and Te Papa Tongawera, the exciting and modern national museum.

The South Island is no less exciting—some people say more so! There are the national parks in the vicinity of Nelson, itself a historical town, there is the rugged West Coast, and there are the spectacular Southern Alps that can be crossed by a tourist train from Christchurch. Then there is Christchurch itself, the garden city of New Zealand that is considered the most 'English' city in the country. Further south is Dunedin, the old Scottish settlement, with splendid buildings built with the money the gold diggers wrested from their claims in the latter part of the 19th century. You can also take a trip out to Taiaroa Heads, across the harbour entrance from the township of Port Chalmers, to visit the only mainland colony of breeding albatrosses. And I haven't even mentioned Queenstown with its backdrop of mountains and historic lake steamer which, incidently, is still doing daily trips for tourists. Finally, in this very cursory overview, there is Milford Sound, the terminus of the famous Milford track that I mentioned in the last section. The picture of Mitre Peak mirrored in the waters of Milford Sound has become one of the icons of New Zealand tourism.

So there is plenty to do and see. We have seen in the last section that sport and recreation are well organised and have a good infrastructure in New Zealand, and I have not even mentioned extreme sports such as bungee jumping (hurling yourself off a bridge or tower with an elastic rope attached to your ankles) which was invented in New Zealand. If it is not to your taste to have an elastic rope attached to your ankles, try hurling yourself out of an aircraft strapped to an experienced parachute jumper; you can do that too in New Zealand. Or else you can go paragliding, soaring up into the sky on a parachute that is towed through the water by jet boat, or hang-gliding off western coast cliffs or mountains.

A cruise through Milford Sound is a pleasant way of taking in the scenery. Mitre Peak is in the background.

A bungee jumper plunges into the depths below.

Have I whetted your appetite? Well, if you are here for some time, you can do all that and much more without having to cram it into a couple of weeks. Mind you, many of our tourists return, sometimes for several years, because they simply can't get enough of New Zealand. Perhaps the Lonely Planet people are right after all!

SOCIAL SECURITY

I recently visited the United States on a business trip. I had to go to a comparatively small city in the South, and as I always do, I bought a local newspaper because they always give you an interesting insight into what is important to the local community. I sat down at a table in a sidewalk café and sipped a cup of excellent coffee while reading the paper and watching the world go by. One of the letters to the editor complained about the lack of patriotism in the community. The writer obviously felt deeply about it. Was America, as he called it, not the freest society in the world, the most powerful, the wealthiest? Indeed, the writer asserted, there was no poverty in America. I looked up from my paper and counted three beggars rattling their paper cups along the main street.

There are no obvious beggars in New Zealand. There are buskers in the street of larger cities, but in many cases these are schoolchildren trying to get a bit of extra pocket money. Of course, we have our share of derelicts and street people, but on the whole they are looked after and don't need to resort to begging. There is a range of both government and community agencies, often staffed by volunteers, who do this work. One way to integrate into the community and to meet a group of locals is to become a volunteer. You can find out about this work through your local Council or the Citizens Advice Bureau.

New Zealand has always been a socially-aware country. Before the arrival of the Europeans, Maori tribal society had mechanisms that ensured that nobody had to go hungry or lacked care. New Zealand was the first country to give women the vote, to adopt the eight-hour working day, and to introduce a universal retirement pension called the Superannuation in New Zealand.

Welfare

Today, a number of welfare benefits are administered by Work and Income New Zealand (WINZ), a government agency that takes a coordinated approach to helping New Zealanders who need work-search, income and in-work support. The agency will assign a case manager to each client, who will then discuss the immediate needs of the clients, and then help them to apply for the appropriate benefits, assess their work skills, arrange for training if necessary, and refer them to employment counsellors. More information is available on the agency's website which is listed in the *Resource Guide*.

One of the main benefits administered by WINZ is the Unemployment Benefit and the Independent Youth Benefit. These are income support payments currently ranging from NZ$107.76 for a single person under 20 years of age living at home, to NZ$161.65 for a single person over 25 years of age. Extra payments are available if the beneficiary has children in his or her care. The benefits apply to New Zealand citizens or permanent residents who have been in the country for at least two years at one time.

A second benefit available through WINZ is New Zealand Superannuation. Every New Zealander or permanent resident, regardless of their financial situation, is entitled to a retirement benefit once they reach age 65. They must, however, have lived in New Zealand for a total of 10 years since they turned 20, and five of these years must have been spent in New Zealand since they turned 50. The payments are made fortnightly and are quite modest. At the time of this writing, a married couple with both partners eligible would get NZ$377.38 each after tax, provided they had no other income. If they have other income, the gross payment would stay the same, but the tax rate would be higher. A single person, living alone with no other income, can expect to get NZ$490.60 per fortnight. Extra payments and benefits are available for medical care, housing and other necessities, but special application has to be made for these to ensure that there is a genuine need for assistance.

The other main benefits administered by WINZ include War Pensions; Invalids Benefit for people who are permanently and severely restricted in their capacity for work because of a sickness, injury or disability; a Sickness Benefit; Widows Benefit; Domestic Purposes Benefit, paid mainly to single parents or caregivers to sick people who need constant care at home; and an Orphans and Unsupported Child's Benefit, paid to the main caregivers of children whose parents cannot support them. A single parent is defined as a parent who has sole responsibility for a dependent child.

HATCHED, MATCHED AND DESPATCHED

In the section on health I have dealt with the technicalities of bringing a baby into the world here in New Zealand. There are however, some social aspects to the process that deserve mention. New Zealanders usually announce the arrival of an offspring by putting an advertisement into the local newspaper. If you have an addition to the family, have a look at the paper to see the style that is used for such advertisements. Usually they include the name of the new arrival, the birth weight and often also thanks to the midwife, doctor and hospital team. Some maternity hospitals, also called 'birthing centres' nowadays, have a website on which you can post photos of the new arrival. Births, incidentally, must be registered with the Registrar of Births, Deaths and Marriages as soon as possible. Normally, the midwife or hospital administrator will hand you a form to fill in. If you don't get one within a week or so, contact the office of the Registrar of Births, Deaths and Marriages, whose website is listed in the *Resource Guide* at the end of this book and ask for one. Registration of a birth is free, although you will be charged a fee (NZ$26 at the time of this writing) if you want a birth certificate.

If one of your friends or workmates or employees has had a baby, they will appreciate receiving a small 'baby gift' to acknowledge the event. Such gifts do not need to be lavish, indeed, if they are too expensive they could cause embarrassment. An item of baby clothing or a small toy is fine. Traditionally, baby girls are dressed in pink, while baby boys wear blue clothes. If you don't know whether the baby is a boy or a girl, choose something multicoloured.

Adolescence

Babies have a habit of growing up and becoming young adults very quickly. They can legally buy and drink alcohol at age 18. If you are around that age, and want to buy some beer or wine in the supermarket, you will need some form of identification (a driver's licence, for example), to prove that you are indeed old enough. The age of majority however, is traditionally 21, and in New Zealand, the 21st birthday is celebrated with particular gusto. Nevertheless, by that age you can already legally buy alcohol, as we have just seen, and you are also already entitled to vote in parliamentary elections. The voting age is also 18. For the 21st birthday, the parents usually put on a party. In the old days, the birthday boy or girl would be handed a large key, symbolic of the fact that he or she would no longer have to ask permission to come and go, but in view of the lower age at which young people are considered to be adults these days, this custom is observed very rarely, if at all.

Getting Married

Once a couple have decided to marry, they announce to their friends that they are engaged. They will do this by placing an advertisement in the newspaper, and the prospective husband, now called fiancé, will buy his bride a ring, often decorated with diamonds, which she will wear on the fourth finger of her left hand. Often, there will also be a party for the immediate friends, and if you are invited, it is usual to bring a small present.

If you are getting married in New Zealand, you will need to find a marriage celebrant and get a marriage licence. Getting a marriage celebrant is no problem. If you are Christian and go to church, your local minister is a licensed marriage celebrant. Secular celebrants are listed in the Yellow Pages of your telephone directory. The licence itself also should present no problems, provided you are not already married, closely related to your proposed partner, or under 16 years of age. (If either party is under 20, the consent of the parents is required). You will also need to have determined when and where you will get married, because you will need that information when you apply for a licence for which, of course, you will be charged a fee.

The licence is important. Without it, there can be no wedding. Many years ago, I was best man for a friend of mine, and on the Friday

A newly-married couple smiles for the camera on their big day.

before the wedding, I took him to have a drink at about 4:30 p.m. As we sat there talking, I asked him whether he had got his marriage licence. He jumped up with a start—he actually had forgotten to obtain it! We jumped into my car and raced across town, breaking all speed limits to get to the court house where the Registrar's office was before it closed at 5:00 p.m. We *almost* made it. At about 5:05 p.m. we screeched to a halt outside the main door and, to our horror, found the doors locked. We ran around the back of the building and found a window open, through which we could see a court official just tidying his desk before leaving for home. When we explained our predicament, he relented, came around the front, opened the door for us and issued the licence. I would not recommend this method of getting a marriage licence!

As I have mentioned in an earlier chapter, the wedding itself is a comparatively modest celebration. A short time before the actual wedding day, some friends of the bride may arrange a 'kitchen evening'. This usually is a women-only party, where the bride is given presents to set up her own kitchen, so kitchen utensils (or even home-made preserves) are suitable gifts for this occasion. If you are invited to the wedding, it is helpful to inquire about presents. Many young couples have gift lists, where they write down suitable gifts in a range of prices to ensure that they don't end up with half a dozen sets of kitchen knives but no toaster.

The men's equivalent of the kitchen evening is the 'stag night', often held on the night before the wedding. It is a men-only party celebrating the last night of 'freedom', and it often is accompanied by all sorts of tricks being played on the hapless bridegroom. In my younger days, I used to occasionally play for weddings in the local Anglican cathedral. I will never forget one wedding on a hot summer's day, when during the service the best man suddenly fell forward, stiff as a ramrod, and had to be revived. A short time later, the bridegroom did exactly the same. The priest interrupted proceedings and motioned to me to play a brief interlude on the organ, while the two young men were fanned and splashed with water. Two chairs were fetched for them and the service took its course. When the priest finally pronounced the couple husband and wife, the pronouncement was greeted with loud cheering and clapping. The two men had obviously had a far too exuberant stag night.

I have already referred to the 'best man' a couple of times. It is usual in New Zealand to have attendants for the bride and groom. There may be one or several, called 'best man' and 'groomsmen' for the bridegroom and 'bridesmaids' for the bride. While you certainly can get married without them, the custom goes back to the middle ages where the bridal couple was treated like nobility for one day.

You can get married without attendants, but you must have at least two witnesses. When I was a student, I used to earn some money playing the organ for weddings in a local church. I remember one wedding where I had received very elaborate instructions about what I had to play at which part of the service. After such a buildup, you can imagine my surprise when at the appointed time, the couple turned up without attendants, without guests—just the two of them! The priest quickly ran across to his home next to the church and fetched his wife from their kitchen. I then played a grand march for the couple's entry into the church. At the appropriate moment, I slipped off the organ bench to go and sign the register as a witness together with the priest's wife, then returned to the organ to play the piece requested by the couple while they paraded down the aisle in solitary splendour!

There are basically two parts to a New Zealand wedding. The first is the formal ceremony, which may be either religious or secular. Unlike in some cultures, the marriage celebrant becomes a government official for the purposes of the ceremony. The register is signed there and no 'civil' ceremony is necessary. The formal part is followed by the wedding 'breakfast', no matter what the time of day. The term 'breakfast' goes back to when the Catholic Church would bless the union with a Mass in the morning. Since the faithful could not take communion if they had already eaten, they would go to church for the wedding, and then assemble to have breakfast.

It is becoming more usual now in New Zealand for wedding celebrations to span a couple of days. The usual day to get married is Saturday. The parents may invite those who have not been formally invited to the actual wedding to an informal lunch meal on Sunday. Usually the bride and groom will still be in attendance. This has probably developed because family and friends can be scattered all over the country and beyond and want to make the most of their time together.

Funerals

If a death occurs in a New Zealand household, customs vary depending on whether it is a Maori or *Pakeha* family. Most New Zealanders will

A traditional cemetery full of tombstones marking the graves of loved ones.

use a funeral director or undertaker to make the arrangements for burial or cremation, and they will also assist with the necessary paperwork for registering the death. With *Pakeha* New Zealanders, it used to be customary for the body to be kept at the undertaker's premises until the funeral. This custom is changing; more and more families elect to have the body in their home. During this time, friends and family will call to express their condolences and take leave of the deceased. If you call at the house, it is a nice gesture to bring some flowers and sometimes some baked goods (such as a cake, muffins or some biscuits) to help the grieving family with the entertaining of the guests.

The formal funeral ceremony is held usually two to three days after the death, either at the funeral home or in a church. The funeral notice in the newspaper will indicate whether to take cut flowers to the service or give a donation to a named charity. The family normally covers the new grave with the flowers or donates them to a hospital or rest home for the elderly if there is a cremation. Nowadays, there often is no public graveyard or crematorium service, and the interment or cremation is attended only by close family members. The grave, which the family buys, will remain the deceased's forever. In some cultures, graves are reused after a certain period. Not so as yet in New Zealand. However, the style of cemetery varies from place to place. Many cities have lawn cemeteries where you may have only flat plaques let into the ground, while other cemeteries have sections to allow graves with monuments erected according to the culture of the family. Cremated ashes may be scattered in accordance with the wishes of the deceased or their family, and a memorial plaque may be inserted in a garden of memories attached to the cemetery.

Maori customs are a bit different and they vary from tribe to tribe, Some traditions however, are generally adhered to. For example, the body is never left alone between death and burial. This is due to the belief that the spirit of the dead hovers around the body for some time and visits its favourite haunts. Once it is released, according to Maori lore, it travels up to the northernmost tip of the North Island and takes leave of the country at Spirits Bay to return to the land of its ancestors.

As soon as possible, and where it is possible, the body is taken to the home *marae* and lies in state in the meeting house, attended around the clock by the family and the *kuia*, the senior women of the tribe. The grave is dug by the male relatives in the local *urupa*, the family cemetery. You will need to be aware that attending the *tangi* of a relative is a very important obligation for a Maori. If you have employees who have to attend, they will be absent from work for several days. There will be a time set for the actual funeral service, and as a non-Maori it is acceptable to just attend for the duration of the service and burial. It would however, be rude not to stay for the meal afterwards. This meal is very important, in that it marks the end of the immediate period of grieving.

The Pacific Island section contains graves that are marked differently from Pakeha *graves.*

If you attend a Maori funeral, you will, as for other occasions, be welcomed onto the *marae* in a group with the formal ceremonial that I have described earlier. If it is a large funeral, there will be many groups to be welcomed, and this can take many hours.

After the ceremonies and the church service are concluded, the coffin is taken to the cemetery and interred, while the mourners gather around the grave until it is filled in. On leaving the cemetery, you will find a container full of water near the gate. Maori sprinkle a little water over themselves to ensure that no evil spirit follows them out.

Deaths are announced by newspaper advertisements. In keeping with the New Zealander's avoidance of ostentation, these are simple, single column advertisements. Some cultures like to show their respect for the deceased by having more elaborate announcements. A few days ago, I saw a nice compromise. The advertisement announced the death of a Samoan woman. In keeping with the New Zealand custom, is was single column, but with a photo and a list of her entire family, it stretched for a respectable 36 cm (14 inches)!

A short period of time after the funeral, the bereaved family may send you an acknowledgement of your attendance at the funeral or for a card or donation you may have sent. Sometimes a thank-you notice will appear in the local newspaper.

If you glance through the family notices in the local paper, you may see advertisements inviting people to attend an 'unveiling'. This is a service in the cemetery, usually a year or more after the funeral of a Maori, to mark the unveiling of the grave stone. It is veiled before sunrise and then the veil is taken off during the ceremony. Just like the *Pakeha* 'in memoriam' notices, the unveiling is a way to remember and pay respect to the dead.

Weddings and funerals are two occasions when New Zealanders tend to wear comparatively formal dress. Unless the wedding invitation states otherwise, it is normal to wear either a suit or a jacket and tie for gentlemen, and elegant daywear for ladies. At a wedding we attended as guests recently, some of the ladies chose to wear hats. This is fine but not required. The only pitfall for ladies is that they do not dress up to the point where they could eclipse the mother of the bride!

SPECIAL REQUIREMENTS FOR NON-NEW ZEALANDERS

When we first arrived in New Zealand, we had to go down to the local police station within a certain time of our arrival to be registered as 'aliens'. The process involved, among other things, having our fingerprints taken, presumably because we were considered to be more likely to commit a crime than New Zealand citizens.

Today, the whole process is much friendlier, although a couple of things have not changed. If you want to apply for a Residence Permit, you must still, as we had to, provide a medical certificate to show that you and any people who apply with you (family members, for example) have an adequate standard of health. A second requirement is a police certificate, because if you have ever been convicted of a crime and sentenced to imprisonment for five years or more, or have

185

been imprisoned for 12 months or more during the 10 years preceding your application, you will be refused residence in New Zealand. The same applies if you have ever been deported from New Zealand or any other country, or if there is reason to believe that you may be associated with a criminal group or constitute a danger to New Zealand. You will appreciate that in these days of increased international terrorist activity, the New Zealand authorities, like authorities in other countries, are particularly vigilant. The third general requirement is that you have to be able to demonstrate that you have sufficient financial means to maintain yourself and any family members that apply with you for the first 24 months in New Zealand.

Visas

If you would like to come to New Zealand to work, you apply for a Residence Visa that allows you to enter New Zealand for the purpose of obtaining a Residence Permit. The categories under which you may apply are: General Skills, Business (there are 4 sub-categories), Family, Family Quota, the Refugee Family Quota, and the Skilled Migrant. Some of the categories are, as their title indicates, quota based, while others operate under a points system, where you are given points for such factors as qualifications, work experience, age and, in the case of the Business categories, business experience and investment funds. For some of the categories, you will have to meet English language requirements. The requirements for the various categories are fairly complex and change from time to time. If you are interested in coming to New Zealand to work, visit the New Zealand Immigration Service website listed in the *Resource Guide* to find the information that applies to your particular situation.

If you would like to come to New Zealand to study, you can apply for a special student visa, the requirements for which are also on the New Zealand Immigration Service website. Under certain circumstances, a student permit will allow you to work part-time while you are studying.

The easiest way to enter New Zealand is on a visitor's permit. At the moment New Zealand has visa waiver agreements with 47 countries, and your travel agent will be able to let you know whether you need a visitor's visa or not. If not, all you have to do is fill in the arrival card that is handed to you prior to landing in New Zealand. A visitor's permit will be issued by the immigration officer at the airport, stating the length of time that you may stay. The permit allows you to stay in New Zealand as a visitor for a total of nine months in an 18-month period, but it can be extended. Again, the New Zealand Immigration Service website is a reliable source of information. They even have application forms online for you to download. Occasionally, the Immigration Department will allow people on a visitor's permit to do some short-term casual work. This is sometimes the case when a fruit harvest has to be brought in and not enough local pickers are available. However, it pays in every case to ensure that this is the case before accepting work.

Once you are in the country, the only obligation you have is to make sure that you comply with the conditions of the particular visa and permit you have —your fingerprints will only be taken if you get into trouble with the police; something I don't recommend.

If you intend to work in New Zealand, you may need to have your qualifications assessed. The government department to do this is the New Zealand Qualifications Authority. For a fee, they will check that the institution that issued the qualification is a bona fide institution, and establish the equivalence with similar New Zealand qualifications. You need to be aware that what they measure is not your personal competence, but rather the standing of the qualification that you hold.

Finally, I would like to emphasize again how important it is that you learn as much English as possible if you intend to work in New Zealand. When I was writing this book, I talked to a young immigrant who had arrived here with his wife and two young children. They are a lovely couple and he is well qualified in information technology. He is very resourceful and has already had one temporary position. He has however missed out for a job as IT helpdesk operator. The reason? His English is not good enough for him to communicate at an appropriate level, often over the telephone, with the people who need his help.

EPILOGUE

We have come to the end of our imaginary journey to and through Aotearoa/New Zealand. You will be aware that this book can contain only a fraction of what can be written about this country. I have however, taken care to select those aspects that will be of immediate use to anybody contemplating moving here for a time.

Yes, you will feel culture shock when you come to New Zealand from your own culture. Yes, you will feel homesick and miss your favourite foods. Yes, you will get depressed sometimes and wonder whether you made the right decision to come here. Hopefully, this book will help you deal with these situations. I have felt all these emotions and have tried to select for you the information that I would have liked to have but often did not. I have also tried to share with you many of the experiences that have helped me, taught me and often given me what I needed to fit into Kiwi society.

You may be in New Zealand only for a short time. I have decided to stay and settle here for the rest of my life. When I now travel in my native Switzerland I thoroughly enjoy being there, but in the end it is New Zealand that I feel homesick for. I have come through culture shock, have adapted, and am now committed to my new home country. That is my journey. May I wish you all the very best on yours!

CULTURAL QUIZ

SITUATION 1

You are invited to a party and have been told to bring a plate. Do you

    A Bring an empty plate?

    B Bring a stack of paper plates?

    C Bring some party food?

    D Bring a dozen bottles of beer?

Comment

C is correct. A 'plate' in this context means a plate with finger food. Your host would probably not object to a few bottles of beer, but the request is for food.

SITUATION 2

You would like to find out what clubs and societies are in your neighbourhood. Do you

A   Ring the police?
B   Visit the local Citizens Advice Bureau?
C   Put an advertisement in the paper?
D   Try and find out from a friend?

Comment

B is correct. The local Citizens Advice Bureau (or sometimes the local public library) will have the information you are looking for. Your advertisement may not bring you the information you really want and your friend may not have all the information either. The police will likely direct you to the nearest Citizens Advice Bureau or library.

SITUATION 3

When your Kiwi workmates tease you in the first few days of you starting work with them, do you

A   Start a court case for harassment
B   Complain to the boss
C   Laugh along with them
D   Resign from the job

Comment

C is correct, provided the teasing is harmless and stops after a while. If it is serious and persistent, then you should complain to the boss and ask him or her to take steps to make it stop. New Zealand human rights legislation provides for protection from harassment.

SITUATION 4

You enter a public office and find that there is a queue of people waiting to get served. You

A Walk to the front of the queue and try to attract the attention of the person serving the public

B Join the queue at the back and wait for your turn

C Walk along the queue and try to negotiate with the people standing in it for a place

D Walk to the front of the queue and tell the person standing at the front that your business is more urgent than theirs

Comment

B is correct in almost every circumstance. If your business really is more urgent, this is often identified when you arrive and measures will be taken to attend to you separately. If not, no matter how impatient you are, take your place and try to relax. Your blood pressure will be all the better for it, and you will be seen as someone who fits into Kiwi culture.

SITUATION 5

Your neighbour's trees and shrubs are growing over the fence into you property. They are a nuisance for you and you would like them cut back. Do you

A Cut them back and throw them into your neighbour's property

B Ring the local council and lodge a complaint

C Ring the neighbour and ask him to cut back the offending branches

D Ask the neighbour whether he minds you cutting back the branches and offer to remove them.

Comment

D is what a 'good neighbour' would do. You are legally entitled to cut any overhanging branches. You are however, not entitled to throw them back into your neighbour's property, although if you discuss the matter amicably, he may well offer to get rid of them. The Council has neither jurisdiction nor any obligations in this case. In almost every case, it is best to go and talk to the neighbour face to face rather than using the telephone.

SITUATION 6

You are a senior executive in the New Zealand branch of your firm. One morning you arrive early and meet a cleaner in the corridor. You

    A   Ignore him

    B   Give him a curt nod

    C   Greet him like you would a colleague

    D   Stop and have a friendly chat

Comment

C is correct, but **D** is even better if you have the time. New Zealand is an egalitarian society, and everybody expects to be treated if not as an equal, then at least with basic courtesy.

SITUATION 7

You have been in the country for just a short time. During a morning tea break, your colleagues get involved in a fairly heated argument concerning internal politics. Do you

    A   Join in and take sides

    B   Listen carefully but don't offer any strong opinion

    C   Tell them how things are done in your country and how much better they are compared to New Zealand

    D   Leave the room

Comment

B is correct, particularly if you have not been in the country very long. Your colleagues may resent being lectured, and if you participate, the ones with whose viewpoint you disagree may regard you (probably rightly) as 'forward', that is offering an opinion without the necessary background. Making comparisons with your home country to the detriment of New Zealand is never a good idea, even though they may be perfectly valid. Leaving the room could create the impression that you are not really interested.

SITUATION 8

You are interviewing a prospective employee. You need the person to work on the occasional Saturday. Do you

    A Ask the person whether they belong to a religion that does not allow them to work on Saturdays

    B Ask the person whether they have family commitments on weekends

    C Ask the person whether they are married

    D Ask the person whether they would be available to work on occasional Saturdays

Comment

D is correct. The other three questions could all be interpreted as an intention to discriminate against the applicant on the grounds of religion, family status or marital status, and you would therefore be in trouble with the New Zealand human rights legislation.

SITUATION 9

You are introduced for the first time to a female Kiwi business partner. You did not quite catch the name when the introductions were made and she has not handed you a business card. Do you

    A Walk up to her and hold out your hand, saying something like, 'pleased to meet you ... (mumble mumble mumble)'

    B Bow and say nothing

    C Go up to her, hand over your business card and ask her for hers.

    D Walk up to her, smile and say that you didn't quite catch her name.

Comment

D is the correct answer. It is polite to wait and see whether the person to whom you are introduced, if she is female, puts out her hand for shaking. If not, a very slight bow (more of a nod, actually) is appropriate, accompanied by a smile. But you still do not have her name. Asking for a business card could cause embarrassment because she may not have one with her. The Kiwi thing to do is to smile and come out with the question at the time of the introduction. If you let the moment pass, you may well have some embarrassment yourself when you have to address her later.

SITUATION 10

One of your Maori staff members asks you for four days' leave because a member of his family has died and he has to attend the *tangi* in a remote part of the country. He has already used up his annual leave entitlement. Do you

    A Give him four days' special leave?

    B Refuse him leave because he has no more days left?

    C Ask him when the actual funeral is and give him just that day off?

    D Dismiss him?

Comment

A is probably the best way to handle this situation. If you use **B**, you may not have to use **D**, because the worker may well resign on the spot. Attending the *tangi* of a family member is a very important duty for Maori, and the obligations are not just limited to attending the actual funeral. Of course, some Maori workers may try and abuse the sensitivity you show and may invent *tangi* when they want a few days off. If you suspect that this is the case, ask to see a death notice to make sure that a relative has indeed died.

DO'S AND DON'TS
APPENDIX

DO'S

- When greeting a New Zealander, do look into his or her eyes, smile and shake the right hand firmly. Kiwis don't enjoy limp (that is weak) handshakes.

- When you are invited out for dinner to a private home, do congratulate the hostess on her cooking. She would have probably prepared the meal herself and will appreciate your compliment.

- If you are standing in a group with one or several New Zealanders at a social function, do give them enough body space. They don't like being 'crowded' by people standing too close to them while having a conversation.

- When you are invited to dinner, do bring along a little present, such as a small box of chocolates, some flowers or a bottle of wine. While this is not mandatory, it will be very much appreciated.

- When you have a business appointment, do arrive on time. New Zealand business people consider lateness to be either rude or a sign that you are not really interested in the contact.

- If you want to go out fishing or gathering seafood, do make sure that you know what the regulations are (and make sure that you stick to them scrupulously). There is enough for everyone as long as the quotas are adhered to.

- Do try and be a good neighbour. (Instructions are given earlier in this book!). It will make your stay in New Zealand so much more pleasant and enjoyable.

- Although New Zealanders generally dress quite casually, do make sure that when you attend business meetings you dress conservatively. It will be appreciated and will help you to make a good first impression.

- If you own or rent a property that has a garden around it, do make sure that you keep it tidy. New Zealanders generally like to have tidy gardens and they appreciate it if their neighbours keep theirs looking nice as well.

DON'TS

- When using a toilet in New Zealand, don't stand on the seat or splash it with water after use. New Zealanders use toilet paper, and even if you prefer to use water (provided it is available), make sure that you leave the toilet clean and dry.

- When you exchange presents with a New Zealand business partner, don't give presents that are valuable. This could be misinterpreted as an attempt to influence the negotiations in your favour.

- Don't ever suggest that New Zealand and Australia are one country or somehow fit into the same category. New Zealanders are very proud of their independent status.

- In a Maori setting, don't ever sit on a table or any other surface where food could be stored or prepared. It is safest to sit only on furniture built specifically for that purpose; chairs or benches (the floor is fine as well).

- In a social setting, don't ever ask a lady her age. This is considered very rude.

- When you are offered food in a Maori setting, don't start to eat until the *karakia* (prayer) has been said.

- When you are at a surf beach, don't ever swim outside the flags that mark the patrolled area. Too many people have drowned because they ignored the flags.

- Don't participate in discussions of sport or politics, particularly if they get heated, until you have been part of the group that is discussing them for some time and have some insight into the issues.

- Don't ask a New Zealander about his or her personal finances, how much they earn, what their personal items cost etc. This is considered rude and will cause embarrassment.

- If you are a smoker, don't smoke in public buildings, and if you are in a restaurant, make sure that there is a smoking section and you are in it before lighting up.

- If you are having dinner, don't put your cutlery on the tablecloth when you have finished. Put them on your plate.

CALENDAR OF FESTIVALS AND HOLIDAYS

NATIONAL PUBLIC HOLIDAYS

New Zealand has a number of national public holidays, some of which coincide with religious festivals.

New Year's Holiday	1–2 January
Waitangi Day (national day)	6 February
Good Friday	
Easter Monday	Dates vary from mid-March to end of April
Anzac Day (war remembrance day)	25 April
Queen's Birthday	1st Monday in June
Labour Day	Last Monday of Oct
Christmas Day	25 December
Boxing Day	26 December

REGIONAL PUBLIC HOLIDAYS

These holidays, which commemorate the 'founding' of a region or province, are always celebrated on a Monday, thus making it a long weekend for people to enjoy. The actual dates are:

Wellington	22 January
Northland and Auckland	29 January
Nelson	1 February
Otago and Southland	23 March
Taranaki	31 March
Hawkes Bay and Marlborough	1 November
Westland	1 December
Canterbury	16 December

On years in which the actual date falls between Tuesday and Thursday, the holiday is observed on the preceding Monday. If it falls between Friday and Sunday, the holiday is observed on the following Monday.

FESTIVALS

This calendar lists only the major events. There are many more local festivals that are advertised in the local press or on tourism websites. Because the exact dates may vary from year to year, only the months are given.

January
- Auckland Anniversary Regatta (Auckland). This is the largest one-day regatta in the world.
- Heineken Tennis Open (Auckland)
- Waipu Annual Highland Games (Waipu, Northland)

February
- Auckland Festival (Auckland)
- Canterbury Wine and Food Festival (Christchurch)
- Central Otago Wine and Food Festival (Queenstown)
- Fringe NZ Festival (Wellington). A showcase of media talents.
- Lake Taupo Arts Festival (biennial, Lake Taupo)
- Marlborough Food and Wine Festival (Blenheim)
- New Zealand International Arts Festival (biennial, Wellington)
- Symphony Under the Stars (Auckland). An open-air concert.
- Waitangi Day celebrations (Bay of Islands, with smaller celebrations elsewhere)
- Wairarapa Wine and Food Festival (Masterton)

March
- Around the Bays Fun Run (Auckland)
- Golden Shears Sheep Shearing Contest (Masterton)
- Hokitika Wild Food Festival (Hokitika) Festival of strange and unusual food.
- International Bill-Fish Tournament (Bay of Islands)
- Ngaruawahia River Regatta (Ngaruawahia, near Hamilton). The only regatta where you will see Maori canoe races, plus much, much more.
- Pasifika Polynesian Festival (Auckland)

April
- Bluff Oyster and Seafood Festival (Bluff)
- Hastings Scottish Highland Games (Hastings)
- Royal Easter Show (Auckland). Originally a pastoral show, it has now expanded to be a large popular trade show.
- Taihape Gumboot Day (Taihape)

May
- Creative Fibre Festival (Masterton)

June
- New Zealand National Field Days (Hamilton). The largest pastoral show in New Zealand with a strong focus on agriculture.

July
- Christchurch Arts Festival (biennial, July/August, Christchurch)
- Queenstown Winter Festival (Queenstown)

September
- Wearable Arts Awards (Nelson)
- The Great Race (Hamilton)

October
- Kaikoura Seafest (Kaikoura)

November
- Rotorua Trout Fishing Tournament

GLOSSARY

A&E	Accident and Emergency department
AA	New Zealand Automobile Association
ACC	Accident Compensation Corporation
All Blacks	The New Zealand national rugby team
Aotearoa	The Land of the Long White Cloud. A Maori name for New Zealand, now widely used by both Maori and non-Maori
ATM	Automatic Teller Machine
bach	holiday cottage
banger	sausage
BBQ	barbecue
bomb	old car in bad condition
booze	alcohol
boozer	pub, bar
break the ice	get to know and be comfortable with people
bro	brother, mate, chum
bun fight	a social gathering where food is served
bush	New Zealand forest
BYO	Bring Your Own (usually alcohol)
champ at the bit	be impatient
cheers	Said when raising your glass to someone, but increasingly used to mean 'thank you'
chillie bin	insulated container for food, usually kept cold by ice pads
chook	chicken
cockie	farmer

cool	smart, clever, pleasing
cracker	Kiwi slang for 'very good indeed'
crib	holiday cottage
crook (n)	criminal
crook (adj.)	sick
put someone crook	give a person the wrong information
dag	humorous person or situation
dags	dried clots of dirt and faeces stuck to a sheep's wool around the tail. When the sheep runs, they make a rattling sound. Hence: rattle your dags means 'Hurry up'
dairy	corner store
DOC	New Zealand Department of Conservation
DPB	Domestic Purposes Benefit (a social welfare payment)
EFTPOS	Electronic Fund Transfer at Point Of Sale
freezing works	meat works, abattoir
GP	general practitioner (medical doctor)
GDP	Gross Domestic Product
good on ya	well done, congratulations
gumboots	black rubber boots
haere mai	welcome
haka	Maori war dance
hakari	feasts
hang back	be reluctant
hangi	meat and vegetables cooked in an earth oven
hapu	sub-tribe
hongi	Maori greeting by pressing noses

hui	meeting, gathering
IRD	Inland Revenue Department
iwi	tribe
just desserts	what a person deserves
JP	Justice of the Peace
kai	food
kainga	unfortified Maori village
karanga	call (of welcome) by women of a Maori tribe
karakia	prayer, grace before meals
kaumatua	Maori elder
kia ora	Maori greeting of 'hello'
kiore	a Polynesian rat introduced to New Zealand by the early Maori settlers
kiwi	flightless bird, one of New Zealand's icons
Kiwi	what New Zealanders call themselves
kiwifruit	a brown fuzzy fruit with bright green flesh and decorative star-shaped seeds. Also known as the Chinese goosberry.
know-all	a person who thinks he knows everything better
koha	gift, present
kohanga reo	literally 'language nest'. Preschools where teaching is through the medium of Maori
kuia	senior woman in a Maori tribe
kumara	sweet potato
loo	toilet, restroom
loot	money, presents
LMVD	Licenced Motor Vehicle Dealer
LTSA	Land Transport Safety Authority

mana	prestige, renown, authority
marae	Maori meeting area that consists of several buildings. It also often refers to the square in front of the Maori meeting house.
MMP	Mixed Member Proportional system. This system is used for New Zealand's parliamentary elections.
moko	facial or body tattoo
MP	member of parliament
NCEA	National Certificate of Educational Achievement
NZQA	New Zealand Qualifications Authority
OE	Overseas Experience. The overseas journey most young Kiwis undertake before settling down in New Zealand
pa	Maori fort, settlement
Pakeha	European
paua	abalone
PAYE	pay as you earn (the New Zealand system of deducting income tax from your wages)
PIN	personal identification number
piss	alcohol
piss around	wasting time
piss-poor	of very low quality
pissed	drunk
pissed off	angry
Plunket nurses	nurses who provide maternity care for mothers and their infants. The Plunkett society is a welfare organisation.
powhiri	formal Maori welcome

puku	stomach
quick on the uptake	a fast learner
rip	a strong tidal current
shark and greasies	fish and chips
shout	pay for someone, usually for a drink
SPCA	Society for the Prevention of Cruelty to Animals
spin a yarn	tell a story
spot on	exactly right
stubby	a small bottle of beer
suss out	figure out, explore
sweet	excellent, fine
TAB	Totalisator Agency Board (The New Zealand betting agency)
take the piss	make fun of, ridicule
tangata whenua	people of the land
tangi	Maori funeral
taniwha	water sprite
taonga	treasure, prized possession
tapu	sacred, forbidden
tena koe	Greetings (to one person)
tena koutou	Greetings (to many people)
tikanga	custom, protocol, way of doing things
tramping	hiking
tupuna	ancestors
umu	earth oven in which the *hangi* is cooked
urupa	Maori family cemetery
waiata	a song, chant or dance

wananga	Maori tertiary institutions specializing particularly in Maori culture
whaka hourua	voyaging canoes
whakapapa	genealogy, family tree
whanau	extended family
whare	house
whare nui	large meeting house
WINZ	Work and Income New Zealand
wop-wops	back country, remote region
yonks	for a long time
yummy	tasty, delicious
zonked out	drunk, stoned, unconscious

RESOURCE GUIDE

ACCIDENT COMPENSATION
Accident Compensation Corporation
http://acc.org.nz/

ACCOMMODATION, BUYING
• General Information
http://www.minhousing.govt.nz/
• Real Estate Institute
http://www.realenz.co.nz
• Real Estate Guide for Immigrants and Overseas Investors
http://www.real-estate-nz.com/

ACCOMMODATION, RENTING
• Ministry of Housing (Tenancy Services)
http://www.minhousing.govt.nz/tenancy

ADVICE, GENERAL
• Citizens Advice Bureau
Freephone 0800 367 222
• Kiwi Ora Programme
http://www.kiwi-ora.com
• New Zealand Immigration Service
http://www.immigration.govt.nz/

Automobile Association see **Cars and Driving**

Births see **Registrar of Births, Deaths and Marriages**

BUSINESS

- Busines Information Zone
  http://www.bizinfo.co.nz
- Chapman Tripp
  http://www.chapmantripp.co.nz/resource_library/
  DoingBusinessInNZ/why.asp
- Commerce Commission
  http://comcom.govt.nz
- New Zealand Companies Office (to register a business)
  http://www.companies.govt.nz
- Ministry of Economic Development
  http://www.med.govt.nz
- Overseas Investment Commission
  http://www.oic.govt.nz
- Statistics New Zealand
  http://www.stats.govt.nz/
- Trade and Enterprise New Zealand
  http://www.tradenz.govt.nz

CARS AND DRIVING

- New Zealand Land Transport Safety Authority
  http://www.ltsa.govt.nz/
- New Zealand Automobile Association
  The association provides a number of services to motorists,
  including breakdown services, vehicle inspection, maps and
  touring itineraries.
  http://www.aa.co.nz.

Citizens Advice Bureau see **Advice, General**

CITIZENSHIP APPLICATIONS

- Department of Internal Affairs
  http://www.dia.govt.nz

COUNSELLING SERVICES
Lifeline telephone counselling Freephone 0800 838 0719
See also **Helplines**.

CONSUMER ADVICE
• Consumer Magazine
 http://www.consumer.org.nz
• Ministry of Consumer Affairs
 http://consumeraffairs.govt.nz

Deaths see **Registrar of Births, Deaths and Marriages**

EDUCATION, SCHOOLING
• Ministry of Education
 Contains a useful directory of institutions
 http://www.minedu.govt.nz
• Education New Zealand
 Provides a wealth of information, particularly for
 foreign students.
 http://www.educationnz.org.nz
• The Correspondence School of New Zealand
 http://www.correspondence.school.nz

EMBASSIES
• New Zealand Ministry of Foreign Affairs and Trade.
 A list of all foreign embassies accredited in New Zealand can
 be found on the website, along with contact information.
 http://www.mft.govt.nz/about/prd/prddefault.html

EMERGENCIES
Dial 111 and ask for the service required:
Police, Fire Brigade, Ambulance, Rescue services

EMPLOYMENT ISSUES
• Employment Relations Service
  http://www.ers.dol.govt.nz
• Human Resource Institute of New Zealand
  http://www.hrinz.org.nz

FERRIES
• Interislander
  http://www.interislandline.co.nz
• Bluebridge ferry
  http://www.straitshipping.co.nz

FILM AND TELEVISION
• Film New Zealand
  http://www.filmnz.com
• Sky Network Television Limited
  http://www.sky.co.nz

FISHING RULES
• Ministry of Fisheries
  http://www.fish.govt.nz

HARASSMENT
• New Zealand Human Rights Commission
  http://www.hrc.co.nz
• abusive phone calls
  If the call involves threat to life, phone 111 for the Police;
  otherwise phone 123

HEALTH
• Ministry of Health
  http://www.moh.govt.nz

• Everybody
> A website for health information.
> http://www.everybody.co.nz

HELPLINES
• Alcoholics Anonymous
> Freephone 0800 229 675
> http://www.alcoholics-anonymous.org.nz
• Alcohol Helpline
> Freephone 0800 787 797
• Gambling Crisis Hotline
> Freephone 0800 654 655

Hiking see **Tramping**

HOSPITALS

Auckland Hospital	(09) 367 0000
Christchurch Hospital	(03) 364 0640
Dunedin Hospital	(03) 474 0999
Waikato Hospital (Hamilton)	(07) 839 8899
Wellington Hospital	(04) 385 5999

For hospitals in provincial centres, please see your local telephone directory for contact information.

IMMIGRATION
• New Zealand Immigration Service
> http://www.immigration.govt.nz

LEARNING ENGLISH
- ESOL Home Tutor Service
   tel (04) 471 2382; email—natoffice@esolht.org.nz;
   fax (04) 271 2383
- Literacy Aotearoa
   http://www.literacy.org.nz

LEGAL SERVICES
- Legal Services Agency
   http://www.lsa.govt.nz
- Office of the Ombudsmen
   http://www.ombusdmen.govt.nz

Marriage see **Registrar of Births, Deaths and Marriages**

MUSEUMS AND ART GALLERIES
- New Zealand Museums Online
   http://www.nzmuseums.co.nz

NATURAL DISASTERS
- Ministry of Civil Defence & Emergency Management
   http://www.civildefence.govt.nz
- New Zealand Institute of Geological and Nuclear Sciences
   http://www.gns.cri.nz

NEW ZEALAND GOVERNMENT
- Government online
   http://www.govt.nz
- House of Representatives (New Zealand Parliament)
   http://www.parliament.govt.nz

Parliament see **House of Representatives**

NEW ZEALAND ENGLISH
• NZ English to US English Dictionary
http://nz.com/NZ/Culture/NZDic.html

NEWSPAPERS ONLINE

Otago Daily Times	http://www.odt.co.nz
The New Zealand Herald	http://www.nzherald.co.nz
Wellington Dominion Post	http://www.dominionpost.com

POSTAL SERVICES
• New Zealand Post
http://www.nzpost.co.nz

QUALIFICATION ASSESSMENT
• New Zealand Qualifications Authority
http://www.nzqa.govt.nz

REGISTRAR OF BIRTHS, DEATHS AND MARRIAGES
http://www.bdm.govt.nz

SPORT AND RECREATION
• Sport and Recreation New Zealand
http://sparc.org.nz

STATISTICS
- Statistics New Zealand
  http://www.stats.govt.nz

TELEPHONE
- New Zealand Telecom
  Freephone 0800 000 000
  http://www.telecom.co.nz
- Online Directories
  http://www.yellowpages.co.nz
  http://www.whitepages.co.nz
- Directory Services
  Calls within New Zealand: dial 018
  International Calls dial 0172 (small fee payable)

TAXES
- Inland Revenue Department (IRD)
  http://www.ird.govt.nz.

TOURISM
- Destination New Zealand
  http://www.destination-nz.com
- Travel and Business
  http://www.newzealand.com
- Lonely Planet guide
  http://www.lonelyplanet.com/destinations/australasia/
  new_zealand

TRAIN
• Tranz Scenic
    http://www.tranzscenic.co.nz

TRAMPING
• Department of Conservation
    http://www.doc.govt.nz

VOLUNTEERING
• Volunteering New Zealand
    Freephone 0800 865 268
    http://www.volunteeringnz.org.nz

WEATHER
• Meteorological Service of New Zealand
    http://www.metservice.co.nz

WELFARE
• Work and Income New Zealand (Ministry of Social Development)
    http://www.winz.govt.nz

WOMEN
• Ministry of Women's Affairs
    http://www.mwa.govt.nz

• National Council of Women
    http://www.ncwnz.co.nz

FURTHER READING

REFERENCE, HISTORY AND NON FICTION

Alexander, Natasha (ed.). *New Zealand: country study guide.*
International Business Publications, Washington D.C., 2000.

Beaglehole, J. C. *The Life of Captain James Cook.* Stanford University
Press, 1983
Arguably the best biography of the great navigator, written by
the scholar who also edited his journals.

Cook, James and J. C. Beaglehole (ed). *The Journals of Captain Cook*
(5 vols). Boydell & Brewer, United Kingdom, 1999.

Fodor's Exploring New Zealand (2nd edition). Fodor's Travel
Publications, 2001

Harding, Paul, Carolyn Bain, Neal Bedford. *New Zealand.* Lonely
Planet Publications, 2002.

Hiora, Te Rangi (Sir Peter Buck), *The Coming of the Maori (2nd
edition).* Whitcoulls Limited, 1987.
Now somewhat dated, the book is still the classic introduction to early
Maori culture in New Zealand and is written by one of the great Maori
scholars of the 20th century.

King, Jane. *Moon Handbooks New Zealand (6th edition).* Avalan
Travel Publishing, 2002.

King, Michael. *The Penguin History of New Zealand*. Penguin, 2003.

New Zealand Official Yearbook. NZ Government Printer.
An annual publication that contains useful statistical information, company and commercial information etc. This information can also be accessed through the website of the Statistics Department.

Rewi, Adrienne. *Frommer's New Zealand*. Frommer, 2002.

Rice, Geoffrey W. (ed). *The Oxford History of New Zealand (2nd edition)*. Oxford University Press, 1994.
An illustrated history of New Zealand.

Robson, John. *Captain Cook's World*. Random House New Zealand, 2000.
A fascinating and comprehensive collection of maps depicting the life and voyages of Captain Cook.

Tauroa, Hiwi. *Te Marae: a Guide to Customs and Protocol*. Reed Books, 2000.
A very useful guide to Maori etiquette.

BIOGRAPHY AND FICTION

New Zealand has a very rich and varied tradition in both fiction and poetry, and an exhaustive bibliography would fill many more pages. I therefore list only a few biographies and autobiographies that seem to me to be of particular interest because of the insights they provide both into the author's or subject's personality, and into the social history of New Zealand. I then list a number of authors whose works have become or are becoming part of the literary 'canon' of New Zealand. You will find them in all New Zealand libraries, and many of their works will also be in libraries in English speaking countries overseas. The list is, of course, not authoritative, it reflects my own personal tastes.

Lauris Edmond

These three volumes are the autobiography of the New Zealand poet
Lauris Dorothy Edmond:
• *Hot October*. Allen & Unwin Port Nicholson Press, 1989.
• *Bonfires in the Rain*. Bridget Williams Books, Wellington, 1991.
• *The Quick World*. Bridget Williams Books, Wellington, 1992.

Janet Frame

Again a trilogy, the autobiography of the novelist Janet Frame. *Angel
at My Table* is also the title of the highly acclaimed film made of Janet
Frame's life and is based on her autobiography.
• *To the Island*. George Braziller,1982.
• *The Envoy from Mirror City*. George Braziller, 1985.
• *Angel at My Table*. Womens Pr Ltd., 2001.

King, Michael. *Frank Sargeson: a Life*. Viking, 1995.
The biography of a major literary figure in 20th century New Zealand
is written by Michael King, one of the country's leading biographer,
writer and historian.

King, Michael. *Te Puea: a Life*. Reed International Books, 2003
The biography of a great Maori leader who made a major contribution
to the renaissance of Maori pride and Maori culture.

King, Michael. *Whina: a Biography of Whina Cooper*. Hodder &
Stoughton, 1983.
Another great Maori *kuia* whose role in the Maori struggle to regain
lands lost after the wars in the 19th century gave her the status of a New
Zealand icon and earned her the respect and affection of both Maori
and *Pakeha*.

King, Michael. *Wrestling with the angel: a life of Janet Frame*.
Viking, 2000

SPORTS AND ENTERTAINMENT

Cycling
Wells, Nicola, Neil Irvine, Ian Duckworth. *Cycling New Zealand.* Lonely Planet, 2000.

Diving
Enderby, Tony and Jenny. *Diving and Snorkelling New Zealand.* Lonely Planet, 2002.

Tramping and Walking
Barnett, Shaun. *North Island Weekend Tramps.* Craig Potton Publishing, 2002

Barnett, Shaun, and Rob Brown. *Classic Tramping in New Zealand.* Craig Potton Publishing, 1999.

Burton, Robert and Maggie Atkin. *A Tramper's guide to National Parks.* Reeds Books, 2001.

DuFresne, Jim. *Tramping in New Zealand (5th edition).* Lonely Planet, 2002.

Hirsh, Walter. *Hidden Trails: 21 Private Walking Tracks in New Zealand.* New Holland Publishers, 2002.

Potton, Criag. *Classic Walks of New Zealand.* Craig Potton Publishing, 1997.

ABOUT THE AUTHOR

 Peter Oettli was born and brought up in Switzerland and received most of his schooling there. He immigrated to New Zealand with his parents, two brothers and a sister when he was in his teens. That is when he experienced the culture shock of coming to New Zealand. At the time, he hardly noticed it; he was too busy being a teenager, but on reflection he has found many instances of it in the period when he became acclimatised to New Zealand society. He finished his secondary schooling and attended university in New Zealand, earning degrees in English and German literature.

After a period doing doctoral research in Germany, he was appointed lecturer in German at the newly founded University of Waikato in Hamilton, where he has worked, in various capacities, ever since. After more than 30 years of teaching, as well as two terms of office as dean of a faculty, he now is Pro Vice-Chancellor (International) at the University. Apart from his professional publications, Peter Oettli has published a book on New Zealand in Switzerland and has also presented a number of radio programmes on New Zealand on the Swiss broadcasting service. His interests include sailing, reading, travelling and video-making (not necessarily always in that order!) He travels widely as part of his current job but at the end of each trip, he is always very happy to return to New Zealand.

Peter Oettli is married and has three grown-up children. He lives with his wife, a cat and, at last count, 22 goldfish, in Hamilton.

INDEX